T0181174

Communications
in Computer and Information Science   2078

Rationale

The CCIS series is devoted to the publication of proceedings of computer science conferences. Its aim is to efficiently disseminate original research results in informatics in printed and electronic form. While the focus is on publication of peer-reviewed full papers presenting mature work, inclusion of reviewed short papers reporting on work in progress is welcome, too. Besides globally relevant meetings with internationally representative program committees guaranteeing a strict peer-reviewing and paper selection process, conferences run by societies or of high regional or national relevance are also considered for publication.

Topics

The topical scope of CCIS spans the entire spectrum of informatics ranging from foundational topics in the theory of computing to information and communications science and technology and a broad variety of interdisciplinary application fields.

Information for Volume Editors and Authors

Publication in CCIS is free of charge. No royalties are paid, however, we offer registered conference participants temporary free access to the online version of the conference proceedings on SpringerLink (http://link.springer.com) by means of an http referrer from the conference website and/or a number of complimentary printed copies, as specified in the official acceptance email of the event.

CCIS proceedings can be published in time for distribution at conferences or as post-proceedings, and delivered in the form of printed books and/or electronically as USBs and/or e-content licenses for accessing proceedings at SpringerLink. Furthermore, CCIS proceedings are included in the CCIS electronic book series hosted in the SpringerLink digital library at http://link.springer.com/bookseries/7899. Conferences publishing in CCIS are allowed to use Online Conference Service (OCS) for managing the whole proceedings lifecycle (from submission and reviewing to preparing for publication) free of charge.

Publication process

The language of publication is exclusively English. Authors publishing in CCIS have to sign the Springer CCIS copyright transfer form, however, they are free to use their material published in CCIS for substantially changed, more elaborate subsequent publications elsewhere. For the preparation of the camera-ready papers/files, authors have to strictly adhere to the Springer CCIS Authors' Instructions and are strongly encouraged to use the CCIS LaTeX style files or templates.

Abstracting/Indexing

CCIS is abstracted/indexed in DBLP, Google Scholar, EI-Compendex, Mathematical Reviews, SCImago, Scopus. CCIS volumes are also submitted for the inclusion in ISI Proceedings.

How to start

To start the evaluation of your proposal for inclusion in the CCIS series, please send an e-mail to ccis@springer.com.

Behrooz Sangchoolie · Rasmus Adler ·
Richard Hawkins · Philipp Schleiss ·
Alessia Arteconi · Adriano Mancini
Editors

Dependable Computing – EDCC 2024 Workshops

SafeAutonomy, TRUST in BLOCKCHAIN
Leuven, Belgium, April 8, 2024
Proceedings

Springer

Editors
Behrooz Sangchoolie (iD)
RISE Research Institutes of Sweden
Borås, Sweden

Rasmus Adler (iD)
Fraunhofer IESE
Kaiserslautern, Germany

Richard Hawkins (iD)
University of York
York, UK

Philipp Schleiss
Fraunhofer IKS
Munich, Germany

Alessia Arteconi (iD)
KU Leuven
Geel, Belgium

Adriano Mancini (iD)
Università Politecnica delle Marche
Ancona, Italy

Università Politecnica delle Marche
Ancona, Italy

EnergyVille
Genk, Belgium

ISSN 1865-0929   ISSN 1865-0937 (electronic)
Communications in Computer and Information Science
ISBN 978-3-031-56775-9   ISBN 978-3-031-56776-6 (eBook)
https://doi.org/10.1007/978-3-031-56776-6

This Springer imprint is published by the registered company Springer Nature Switzerland AG
The registered company address is: Gewerbestrasse 11, 6330 Cham, Switzerland

Paper in this product is recyclable.

Preface

The European Dependable Computing Conference (EDCC) is a unique forum for researchers and practitioners to present and discuss their latest research results on theory, techniques, systems, and tools for the design, validation, operation, and evaluation of dependable and secure computing systems. The 19th edition of EDCC was held in Leuven, Belgium, from 8th of April 2024.

Traditionally half- or one-day workshops precede the main conference. The purpose of the workshops is to provide a forum for exchanging opinions, presenting novel ideas, and discussing preliminary results in an interactive atmosphere. In this edition of the conference, the workshops were held on Monday, 8th of April.

Four workshop proposals were submitted to this edition of the conference and, after an evaluation process led by the workshop chair, all of them were accepted. One of these workshops was later cancelled by the organizers of the workshop. The evaluation criteria for the workshops selection included (but were not limited to) the relevance to EDCC, the timeliness, expected interest in the topic, the workshop's potential for generating useful results, and the Organizers' ability to lead a successful workshop.

These joint proceedings include the accepted papers from two of the three workshops. These workshops are:

- 1st Workshop on Safe Autonomous Systems (SafeAutonomy);
- 1st Workshop on the Role of TRUST in the Implementation of Digital Technologies: Blockchain Technology and Artificial Intelligence in Smart Cities (TRUST IN BLOCKCHAIN).

These two workshops received a total of 14 submissions. Each workshop had an independent Program Committee, which was in charge of reviewing and selecting the papers submitted to the workshop. Both workshops adopted a single-blind review process. All the workshop papers received at least two reviews per paper. Out of the 14 submissions, 13 papers were selected to be presented at the workshops and all of these 13 papers are included in these proceedings.

The TRUST IN BLOCKCHAIN workshop accepted extended abstract submissions, whereas the SafeAutonomy workshop accepted regular technical papers, case studies, PhD forum papers, as well as position papers.

I would like to express my gratitude to all those who contributed to the success of the *EDCC workshops day* of this 19th edition of the EDCC conference. First, I thank all the workshops organizers for their dedication and commitment, the authors who contributed to this volume, the reviewers for their help in the paper assessment and the workshops participants.

I would also like to thank all the members of the EDCC Steering committee and Organizing committee, in particular Geert Deconinck (the General Chair) for the smooth communication and his hard work on organizing the conference. A special thank you to Tohid Behdadnia (the Web Chair) for following up on all my requests on updating the conference website and Felicita di Giandomenico (the Publicity Chair) for her support on dissemination of the calls.

Finally, many thanks to the staff of Springer, who provided professional support through all the phases that led to this volume.

February 2024   Behrooz Sangchoolie

Organization

EDCC Steering Committee

Karama Kanoun (Chair)	LAAS-CNRS, France
Juan Carlos Ruiz (Chair)	Technical University of Valencia, Spain
Jean-Charles Fabre	LAAS-CNRS, France
Felicita Di Giandomenico	Institute ISTI, Italy
Johan Karlsson	Chalmers University of Technology, Sweden
Henrique Madeira	Universidade de Coimbra, Portugal
Miroslaw Malek	Università della Svizzera Italiana, Switzerland
Janusz Sosnowski	Warsaw University of Technology, Poland
Michael Paulitsch	Intel, Germany
Alexander Romanovsky	Newcastle University, UK

EDCC 2024 Organization

General Chair

Geert Deconinck	KU Leuven, Belgium

Program Committee Chair

Marcello Cinque	Federico II University of Napoli, Italy

Web Chair

Tohid Behdadnia	KU Leuven, Belgium

Local Organizers

Emilio José Palacios-García	KU Leuven, Belgium
Fairouz Zobiri	KU Leuven, Belgium

Workshops Chair

Behrooz Sangchoolie	RISE Research Institutes of Sweden, Sweden

Students Forum Chair

Simona Bernardi   University of Zaragoza, Spain

Fast Abstracts Chair

Tommaso Zoppi   University of Florence, Italy

Posters Chair

Jeroen Boydens   KU Leuven, Belgium

Publication Chair

Matthias Eckhart   University of Vienna, Austria

Publicity Chair

Felicita di Giandomenico   CNR Pisa, Italy

Liaison Chair

François Vallée   University of Mons, Belgium

Finance Chair

Fairouz Zobiri   KU Leuven, Belgium

Workshop Editors

Workshops Chair

Behrooz Sangchoolie   RISE Research Institutes of Sweden, Sweden

SafeAutonomy

Rasmus Adler   Fraunhofer IESE, Germany
Richard Hawkins   University of York, UK
Phillipp Schleiß   Fraunhofer IKS, Germany

TRUST IN BLOCKCHAIN

Alessia Arteconi   KU Leuven, Belgium
Adriano Mancini   Università Politecnica delle Marche, Italy

Contents

TRUST IN BLOCKCHAIN Short Paper

Workshop on Safe Autonomous Systems (SafeAutonomy)

Workshop on Safe Autonomous Systems (SafeAutonomy)

Workshop Description

The SafeAutonomy workshop explores concepts, techniques and technology related to the continuous safety assurance of autonomous systems (AS). Related previous workshops ran under the name DREAMS (Dynamic Risk managEment for Autonomous Systems) and focused on dynamic risk management of AS. This remains an important aspect of safety assurance for AS, but the SafeAutonomy workshop welcomes a broad range of contributions in any related area. AS have enormous potential to transform society. The key trait of AS is their ability to pursue and achieve their goals independently and without human guidance or intervention. In contexts where safety needs to be guaranteed, it is difficult currently to exploit autonomous systems to their full potential due to the difficulty in providing assurance they will be safe throughout operation. The assurance challenge increases when AS take advantage of Machine Learning to cope with the complexity of their mission and the operating context, and when assuring AS in the context of systems of systems, where emergent behaviours and dynamic composition must be considered.

The SafeAutonomy workshop explored a range of topics related to continuous safety assurance of AS including but not limited to dynamic risk management, situational awareness, resilience, human machine interaction, uncertainty management, assurance cases, virtual validation and safety assessment.

It invited experts, researchers and practitioners for presentations and in-depth discussions about assuring autonomy, its relevance for specific use cases, its relation to existing regulatory frameworks and standardization activities, and solutions from systems and software engineering.

SafeAutonomy aimed to bring together communities from diverse disciplines, such as safety engineering, runtime adaptation, predictive modelling and control theory, and from different application domains such as automotive, healthcare, manufacturing, agriculture and critical infrastructures.

Organization

Program Chairs

Rasmus Adler   Fraunhofer IESE, Germany
Richard Hawkins   University of York, UK
Philipp Schleiß   Fraunhofer IKS, Germany

Program Committee

Karl-Erik Arzen   Lund University, Sweden
Patrik Feth   Psiori, Germany
Martin Fränzle   Carl von Ossietzky Universität Oldenburg,
                              Germany
Andrey Morozov   University of Stuttgart, Germany
Ganesh Pai   KBR/NASA Ames Research Center, USA
Patrik Feth   Sick AG, Germany
Davy Pissoort   Katholieke Universiteit Leuven, Belgium
Ioannis Sorokos   Fraunhofer IESE, Germany
Martin Törngren   KTH, Sweden
Ran Wei   University of Cambridge, UK

Providing Evidence for the Validity of the Virtual Verification of Automated Driving Systems

Birte Neurohr[1]([envelope])[iD], Thies de Graaff[1][iD], Andreas Eggers[2], Tom Bienmüller[2], and Eike Möhlmann[1][iD]

[1] German Aerospace Center (DLR), Escherweg 2, 26121 Oldenburg, Germany
{Birte.Neurohr,Thies.Degraaff,Eike.Moehlmann}@dlr.de
[2] BTC Embedded Systems AG, Gerhard-Stalling-Straße 19, 26135 Oldenburg, Germany
{Andreas.Eggers,Tom.Bienmueller}@btc-embedded.com

Abstract. With the increasing complexity of automated driving systems, formal verification as well as statistical verification that solely relies on real-world testing methods, become infeasible. Virtual testing seems like a promising alternative to traditional methods, especially as part of a scenario-based verification and validation methodology. But in order to transfer the test results of a system from a simulation to the real world, we need to argue the validity of the virtual tests. Our proposed method enables this validity argumentation by comparing the virtual test traces against traces that have sufficiently similar recorded real-world traces. To reduce the amount of required real-world data, the method involves two mechanisms to generalize the validity statement of a single real-world trace to a set of virtual traces. The reduction of required data is showcased in a proof of concept that compares the needed amounts of data with a "naive" validation method and here presented enhancements in an ablation study.

Keywords: Automated Driving · Automated Driving Systems · Computer Simulation · Simulation-based Testing · Validity · Virtual Testing · Virtual Validation

1 Introduction

Automated driving systems (ADSs) [16] are not only thought of as a way to make traveling more comfortable but also as a tool to make it safer [7]. To realize this, it is hence very important to guarantee their safe operation. However, not only the ADSs themselves are highly complex but also the perceived environment which acts as input for such systems. Thus, their careful verification and validation is of high importance. This cannot be done solely with exhaustive (formal) methods as the environment bears infinitely many characteristics, possible interactions and effects [11]. However, when "only" using tests, the number of test kilometers necessary for a statistical evidence of the system's safety amounts to (depending on assumptions/type of accident) several hundreds of millions of kilometers [21] (for comparison: all streets in the US amount to 6.59 million kilometers [2]). In theory, these tests would need to be performed with

B. Sangchoolie et al. (Eds.): EDCC 2024 Workshops, CCIS 2078, pp. 5–13, 2024.
https://doi.org/10.1007/978-3-031-56776-6_1

every newly developed or even slightly modified (e.g. updated) ADS. Hence, this app-roach is infeasible due to constraints on costs and time [8]. A potential solution to this dilemma is to replace physical components with virtual ones mimicking the behavior of their physical counterparts. If part of the testing of an ADS shall be performed in the simulation, one has to provide plausible evidence that the simulation environment is suf-ficiently similar to the real world in the required aspects [9]. Otherwise, any argument obtained from the simulation cannot contribute to a safety assessment in reality. This sufficiently realistic behavior is traditionally called model validation: "substantiation that a computerized model within its domain of applicability possesses a satisfactory range of accuracy consistent with the intended application of the model" [19]. To be able to show this validity, typically, the ADS' performance in the virtual world is com-pared to its performance in the real world while executing the same scenario [1]. But since this does not reduce the amount of needed real-world tests, this method might just be helpful during the development phase, where simulations could already be carried out for a faster and cheaper feedback loop.

In this work, we present a snippet based trace validation method that can reduce the required real-world data for virtual ADS verification. Here, a *trace* is a time series of (multidimensional) simulator states $s_l \in S$, where S is the state space of the simulator. Snippet based trace validation helps to decide if a single trace generated by a simulation can be determined "valid". Note that this is different from traditional model validation as we do not determine a priori a model to be valid but only look at single outputs of the simulation platform (a trace). The general strategy is based on a set of validated simulation traces, for which comparable real-world counterparts were gathered. We then generalize the validity statement of a "known" simulation trace to "new" traces, which we have not already seen in reality by arguing carefully over similarities and recombination. Not having to record every slight variation of a scenario in the real world, our method paves a way towards affordable valid virtual testing of ADSs.

To sum up, this paper contributes to answering the following research question: **How can the amount of needed real world data for the validation of simulated traces be decreased?** To answer this question we

- present a method to validate simulation traces based on real world data,
- propose two enhancements via decomposition and recombination of real world data along (1) time and so called (2) validity aspects, and finally
- demonstrate the effectiveness of these enhancements.

The paper is structured as follows: we start with referring to related work in the field of model validation in Sect. 2. After that, we describe the method and its individual parts in detail in Sect. 3, which will then be applied in our proof of concept in Sect. 4. We conclude this paper with a short summary and an outlook on future work in Sect. 5.

2   Related Work

Validation of computerized models has been a widely recognized problem across multi-ple disciplines since the beginning of their existence. Even though this paper only looks at single simulation traces and hence not directly talks about model validation, these concepts are related as the here presented method may be used to e.g. create a statistical hypothesis test and thus do model validation.

An overview over the topic of model validation, not specific to any application domain is done by Sargent [17], while Oberkampf et al. present the state of the art in the validation of computational physics models [10]. They conclude that, because erroneous conclusions based on modeling and simulation may have disastrous outcomes, it is important to drastically improve the confidence and understanding in computational simulations. The general challenges to determine the degree of model validity are also relevant to the validity of virtual ADS verification. However, in this context the topic has not mainly been addressed for the simulation of vehicle dynamics or sensors.

Viehof proposes a method for a requirement based validation concept in vehicle dynamics simulation [20]. He proposes different validation level where the first one is *statistical sample validity*. The method presented in this paper can be seen as being on this sample layer. With some modifications, this method was applied to an idealized radar sensor model by Rosenberg et al. [15]. However, they reported several challenges (e.g., find more appropriate metrics). In a follow up paper, Rosenberg at al. present a suggestion for a more appropriate metric for the validation of sensor models [14]. However, the extrapolation from the validated samples is still limited.

Schaermann also proposes a validation method for sensor models [18]. As the approaches before, he relies on re-simulation of real world data. He also addresses different levels for sensor model validation: raw data vs. object level.

Riedmaier et al. present a unified framework and survey for model verification, validation and uncertainty quantification [12]. They applied their framework to a *Lane Keeping Functional Test* and assessed the validity via a minimum distance'to line' [13]. This framework was tailored for statistical validation with a focus on uncertainty, e.g. arising from the input data by Danquah et al. [4,5]. In their approach, an extrapolation from validation scenarios is also considered and solved by uncertainty learning and prediction which leads to a quite high prediction uncertainty. In contrast to the aforementioned work, where an extrapolation is done via statistical arguments, the here presented method is based on a generalization.

3 Snipped Based Trace Validation

Demonstrating the validity of all simulation traces a simulator can generate is hard, especially in the automotive context, where we encounter a highly diverse environment with myriads of possible variations, commonly referred to as the open world problem [3]. This is why we reduce the complexity of the validation problem here by assessing the validity for single simulation traces. Those validated simulation traces can then be used during testing in order to reduce the amount of real world testing. In the following we delineate the basic process, which will be extended subsequently to enable a broader application of the method and, thus, increase its usefulness.

3.1 Naive Validation of Simulation Traces

The naive approach of validating a single simulation trace follows a simple idea: If you can find a trace from the real world that is similar enough to the one you have

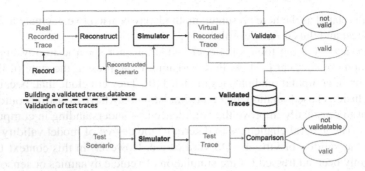

Fig. 1. Naive validation process. Black rectangular boxes represent the process steps, while blue sharp boxes represent artifacts. The process is divided into two phases. (Color figure online)

seen in the simulation, you may conclude that it is a valid trace. If we assume that all relevant information can be observed and, that it is sufficient to observe the validity at the sampling rate of the ADS, similar enough real and simulated data indicate that the simulation trace can be used as a replacement of the real-world trace.

This idea leads to a two-phase process: First (Fig. 1, upper half), one needs to record data in the real world with a sensor-equipped vehicle (e.g., cameras, radars, lidars, CAN bus data), resulting in a *real recorded trace (RRT)*, which is a time series of all measurements. The sensor-equipped vehicle may be driven by a human or an ADS. The RRT is used to reconstruct simulation-suitable representations of the scenery and the scenario. These files have to describe all relevant properties of the real recorded trace, so that it can be replayed by the simulator in the next step. By gathering similar measurements from the simulation as those obtained in the real-world drive, the replay results in a *virtual recorded trace (VRT)*. In the *Validate* step, the RRT and the VRT are compared against each other. If they are not similar enough, the VRT is considered to be invalid and there must be an error either in the scenario reconstruction or in the simulator setup that should be fixed. In case of sufficient similarity, the VRT is valid and added to the *Validated Traces* database. If one is now interested in testing an ADS using a test scenario in the simulator (Fig. 1, lower half), we compare the resulting test trace against the validated traces in the database. If the test trace is not similar enough to an already validated trace, we cannot argue about the validity of the test trace (i.e., it can not be validated at this point), since real-world data might simply be missing. But if a match can be found, the simulative test result is valid. Only comparing the traces is enough, if we assume that the simulator is deterministic and executes the semantic of the scenarios description.

Note that, since the validity of simulation traces is based on the RRT, there exists a coupling between the validity and the modalities of the recording campaign (e.g., sensor setup, vehicle dynamics, ...). When deploying a virtually tested ADS, the physical vehicle has to match those modalities of the recording campaign, otherwise the test results can not be transferred to reality. This restriction stems from the purely data-based nature of our validation process. If adjustments to the physical vehicle are made and one can argue, that those adjustments either have no impact on all measurable properties, or that those adjustments are correspondingly reflected in the simulation model, then this restriction could be relaxed.

3.2 Slicing of Traces by Validity Aspects

In order to accurately reflect the real world, a simulator must include all the relevant aspects of the real world, together with their relations. In the context of ADS, examples for these aspects are the used sensors or the vehicle dynamics. Some of these aspects might work independently from each other, e.g., a radar may be independent from a lidar sensor, due to their different frequencies. We call these independent aspects *validity aspects (VA)*, which can be implemented in the simulation as standalone modules, while only relying on the commonly shared simulation state. Please note, that these aspects have to be chosen *very* carefully (e.g., not all modules in a simulation can automatically be VAs). If there are no independent aspects, then there is just one VA that includes everything. A VA does not have to depend on every variable in the scenario (e.g., objects, daytime, weather conditions) but only on a subset, the so-called *key variables*. For example, a long-range front radar is independent from objects that are not in its field of view, therefore these objects are not part of the key variables of this radar VA (visualized in Fig. 2). We refer to such a reduced trace as *pattern*, which now builds the basis for the comparison of a test trace against the validated traces. A trace of length l $\begin{smallmatrix} s_{0,0} & \cdots & s_{0,l} \\ \cdots & \cdots & \cdots \\ s_{n,0} & \cdots & s_{n,l} \end{smallmatrix} \in S$ is split into traces of a VA

$\begin{smallmatrix} va_{0,0}^j & \cdots & va_{0,l}^j \\ \cdots & \cdots & \cdots \\ va_{m,0}^j & \cdots & va_{m,l}^j \end{smallmatrix}$ and reduced to key variables. This is called a pattern of a VA j $\begin{smallmatrix} k_{0,0}^{va_j} & \cdots & k_{0,l}^{va_j} \\ \vdots^{va_j} & \cdots & \vdots^{va_j} \\ k_{r,0}^{va_j} & \cdots & k_{r,l}^{va_j} \end{smallmatrix}$,

where $n \geq m \geq r \in \mathbb{N}$. Since a pattern drops unnecessary variables for this VA, it can now generalize to a lot more traces. And the more variables can be dropped, the better this generalization ability is. However, when identifying key variables for a validity aspect, we recommend to start with all available variables as key variables, and then remove those variables, which are *sure* to be irrelevant for the VA e.g., with a sensitivity analysis. If no error was made, no incorrect generalization can occur.

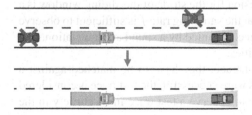

Fig. 2. Visualization of the reduction to key variables for a long-range front radar. Objects outside the field of view and the color of the vehicle can be removed.

When replaying the RRTs, their corresponding VRTs have to be valid w.r.t. all VAs, i.e., the simulator accurately represents the real world in every aspect for each RRT. But when now simulating a test trace and performing its validation, we do not have to find a validated trace in our database that completely matches the new trace, but we can find patterns originating from different validated traces to validate each VA individually. This way, a limited database of validated traces can be used to validate a lot more test traces, reducing the effort for real data acquisition. However, when arguing that these patterns together now form a validated trace great care has to be taken. On an information level there may be emergent behavior that gets lost when only looking at parts. In this case, splitting into validity aspects is prohibited. Moreover, the coupling of the VAs may introduce timing effects that are different in simulation and in reality (eg. FMUs for Co-simulation vs CAN bus in a real vehicle).

Example: Assume we consider two VAs "front camera" and "rear camera". If we recorded two traces in the real world, where 1) the ego vehicle follows another car and 2) the ego vehicle is followed by another car, then for a new test trace where both cases occur at the same time, we can take both existing validated traces to validate the different VAs and therefore the whole test trace.

3.3   Slicing of Traces by Time

When a camera is taking an image, only the light that hits the sensor during its exposure time influences the resulting picture. Analogously, the measurements of active sensors like radar or lidar depend only on the time span between the emission of a ray and its detection. These observations motivate the definition of a maximal time frame – we call it *history* of length τ – in which changes of variables have an effect on a VA at timestep t. The history of each VA might be influenced by some individual factors, e.g., for the environment VA, physical laws are of major relevance. For the sensor VAs, deriving the length of the history might be as easy as looking up the technical specifications. In general, for each VA one has to examine all the relevant causal chains and their respective lengths. The longest relevant causal chain for a VA determines its minimal history length. After deriving the appropriate histories for all VAs, the patterns for each VA can be time-sliced into even smaller chunks with the length of their histories τ, using a sliding window approach. Since the originating patterns of these snippets were already validated, the resulting snippets are referred to as *validity snippets*.

In order to validate a test trace with these validity snippets, the test trace has to be sliced by VAs first and then by time using the same key variables as they were used during the elicitation of the validity snippets. It is very important, that the sliding window must use a stride so that consecutive snippets of the test trace overlap with each other, since otherwise discontinuities could arise, which should not be considered valid (e.g., teleporting vehicles). A safe decision for the stride of the sliding window is a single time step $\Delta t = \frac{1}{f}$, since we assume that the sampling rate f is sufficient to observe the validity. Using a greater stride must be accompanied by a sound argumentation, that this cannot lead to unreasonable discontinuities.

Having collected all snippets of the test trace, they have to be matched against a validity snippet and only if all these matches were successful, the test trace is considered to be valid. By doing so, it is not necessary to observe a test trace in its entirety in the real world, but just its individual parts.

4   Proof of Concept

To showcase the effectiveness of the different presented techniques (*slicing by VA* and *slicing by time*), we performed an ablation study to quantify the amount of required validated traces to validate a set of test traces. For the sake of simplicity, in this case we only assume the validated traces to be valid without having comparable real world data as we focus on the second phase of the presented method. For this, we used the simulator CARLA 0.9.13 [6] and designed a parameterizable highway scenario, where the ego vehicle is following its lane with a desired target velocity $v_e \in [V_{MIN}, V_{MAX}]$, while adapting to its traffic ahead. The initial position is set to the midpoint of a straight highway, but can be longitudinally varied with an offset $o_e \in [-O_{MAX}, O_{MAX}]$. $n_o \in [N_{MIN}, N_{MAX}]$. Other vehicles with target velocity $v_{o,i} \in [V_{MIN}, V_{MAX}], i = 1 \ldots n_o$ are randomly sampled around the ego vehicle, also adapting their velocities to other traffic, while additionally having the option to perform a lane change, if this is enabled ($lc \in \mathbb{B}$).

Table 1. Overview of parameter ranges for different benchmarks

	N_{MIN}	N_{MAX}	V_{MIN} [km/h]	V_{MAX} [km/h]	O_{MAX} [m]	lc
easy	0	3	80	80	100	0
medium	0	5	80	90	150	1
complex	0	10	60	100	500	1

Based on this parameterizable scenario, we derived three benchmarks *easy*, *medium* and *complex* which differentiate by the used parameter ranges (see Table 1). We sampled 200 and 5000 scenarios for each benchmark as test and validated traces.

We implemented the different validation schemes (*naive*, *slicing by VA*, *slicing by time*, *slicing by VA + time*) and evaluated the overall amount of test traces that can be validated in each benchmark. We used a front-looking and a rear-looking camera as well as the ego vehicle dynamics as validity aspects. The patterns for the VAs of the cameras are reduced to the visible objects at each timestep of the trace. To develop an estimate of how the amount of validatable test traces scales with the amount of validated traces, we performed the evaluation on different database sizes. The results are depicted in Fig. 3 and indicate that the different enhancements introduce a great benefit to the amount of validated test traces. The snippet based trace validation is capable of validating 1.7–2.2x more test traces than the naive method. In the *easy* setting, nearly 60% of all test traces can be validated, but the performance drastically reduces for the harder benchmarks, due to the combinatorial complexity of all possible variations.

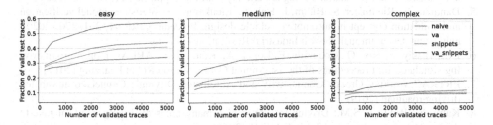

Fig. 3. Results of validating the test traces in the different benchmarks.

5   Conclusion and Future Work

The here presented snippet based trace validation provides evidences for the validity of simulation traces, in order to enable the transfer of virtual testing results to the real world while reducing the amount of needed real world data. It relies on generalizing from traces that were observed in reality and validly replayed in the simulation (the validated traces). Our proof of concept exemplary showed, that our different strategies help to increase the generalization of observed scenarios to multiple similar scenarios. The approach should be applied with great care as wrongfully declared valid traces, have the potential to lead to catastrophic events. This is why research in this area is especially important.

Furthermore, the presented method comes with several limitation. The problems of coupling introduced in Sect. 3.2 will need further investigation as the introduced timing effects may affect the overall validity. Defining good similarity measures for traces are a further topic of interest. An additional step may be needed to include emergent behavior. Furthermore, our proof of concepts only looks at sensor related validity aspects. The usefulness for other validity aspects needs to be examined further.

In order to benchmark our method, we plan to extend our simulative proof of concept to a broader scale and apply it to actual real-recorded scenarios, thus being able to give estimates on the efficiency of snippet based trace validation in a real-world setting. Here, it will be especially interesting how the combinatorial complexity will affect the performance. To make use of real world data the trustworthiness of data also has to be considered.

Acknowledgments. This work has received funding by the German ministries BMWK and BMBF within the projects "KI Wissen"and "ASIMOV".

References

1. ISO 19364 - Passenger cars - Vehicle dynamic simulation and validation-Steady-state circular driving behaviour. Technical report, International Organization for Standardization
2. The world factbook, Washington, DC 20505 (2019)
3. Bendale, A., Boult, T.: Towards open world recognition. In: Proceedings of the IEEE Conference on Computer Vision and Pattern Recognition (CVPR) (2015)
4. Danquah, B., Riedmaier, S., Meral, Y., Lienkamp, M.: Statistical validation framework for automotive vehicle simulations using uncertainty learning. Appl. Sci. **11**(5), 1983 (2021)
5. Danquah, B., Riedmaier, S., Rühm, J., Kalt, S., Lienkamp, M.: Statistical model verification and validation concept in automotive vehicle design. Procedia CIRP **91**, 261–270 (2020). enhancing design through the 4th Industrial Revolution Thinking
6. Dosovitskiy, A., Ros, G., Codevilla, F., Lopez, A., Koltun, V.: CARLA: an open urban driving simulator. In: Proceedings of the 1st Annual Conference on Robot Learning (2017)
7. ERTRAC Working Group "Connectivity and Automated Driving": Connected automated driving roadmap (2019)
8. Kalra, N., Paddock, S.M.: Driving to safety: how many miles of driving would it take to demonstrate autonomous vehicle reliability? (2016)
9. Neurohr, C., Westhofen, L., Henning, T., de Graaff, T., Möhlmann, E., Böde, E.: Fundamental considerations around scenario-based testing for automated driving. In: 2020 IEEE Intelligent Vehicles Symposium (IV), pp. 121–127 (2020)

10. Oberkampf, W.L., Trucano, T.G., Hirsch, C.: Verification, validation, and predictive capability in computational engineering and physics. Appl. Mech. Rev. **57**(5), 345–384 (2004)
11. Poddey, A., Brade, T., Stellet, J.E., Branz, W.: On the validation of complex systems operating in open contexts (2019)
12. Riedmaier, S., Danquah, B., Schick, B., Diermeyer, F.: Unified framework and survey for model verification, validation and uncertainty quantification. Arch. Comput. Methods Eng. **28**, 2655–2688 (2021)
13. Riedmaier, S., Schneider, J., Danquah, B., Schick, B., Diermeyer, F.: Non-deterministic model validation methodology for simulation-based safety assessment of automated vehicles. Simul. Model. Pract. Theory **109**, 102274 (2021)
14. Rosenberger, P., Schunk, G., Ikemeyer, F., Duong, Q.T.: Validation of Test Infrastructure - from cause trees to a validated system simulation
15. Rosenberger, P., et al.: Towards a generally accepted validation methodology for sensor models - challenges, metrics, and first results. In: Graz Symposium Virtual Vehicle (GSVF) (2019)
16. SAE International: Taxonomy and Definitions for Terms Related to Driving Automation Systems for On-Road Motor Vehicles. Technical report
17. Sargent, R.G.: Verification and validation of simulation models. In: Proceedings of the 2011 Winter Simulation Conference (2011)
18. Schaermann, A.: Systematische Bedatung und Bewertung umfelderfassender Sensormodelle. Ph.D. thesis
19. Schlesinger, S., et al.: Terminology for model credibility. SIMULATION **32**(3), 103–104 (1979)
20. Viehof, M.: Objektive Qualitätsbewertung von Fahrdynamiksimulationen durch statistische Validierung. Ph.D. thesis
21. Wachenfeld, W., Winner, H.: Die Freigabe des autonomen Fahrens. In: Maurer, M., Gerdes, J., Lenz, B., Winner, H. (eds.) Autonomes Fahren, pp. 439–464. Springer Vieweg, Berlin, Heidelberg (2015). https://doi.org/10.1007/978-3-662-45854-9_21

What Level of Power Should We Give an Automation?

—Adjusting the Level of Automation in HCPS —

Mehrnoush Hajnorouzi[1]([✉]), Astrid Rakow[1], Akhila Bairy[2],
Jan-Patrick Osterloh[1], and Martin Fränzle[2]

[1] Institute of Systems Engineering for Future Mobility, German Aerospace Center
(DLR) e.V., Oldenburg, Germany
{mehrnoush.hajnorouzi,astrid.rakow,jan-patrick.osterloh}@dlr.de
[2] Carl von Ossietzky Universität Oldenburg, Oldenburg, Germany
{akhila.bairy,martin.fraenzle}@uni-oldenburg.de

Abstract. The level of automation in human-centered systems is steadily increasing, leading to a demand for advanced design methods for automation control at the human-machine interface. This is particularly important in safety-critical applications, where the multi-faceted interaction between the automated system and humans must be carefully analyzed to identify potential risks to the overall safety. This paper presents our vision of an approach determining an appropriate level of automation taking into account the automation's impact on the human. The approach is based on a game theoretic framework where we investigate whether the automation's controller can be synthesized as a strategy considering human behavior and thus ensuring human-adaptive control.

1 Introduction

The increasing automation of human-centered cyber-physical systems (HCPS) requires advanced control technologies that not only control technical tasks, but must also interact with and support users. Adaptation to the users' explicit requirements and implicit needs is important for these systems on the one hand, but on the other hand they must not hinder users. Reconciling these goals is particularly intricate in safety-critical domains. Safety cannot be treated as an ad hoc measure but, as emphasized by Bowen, "safety must be designed into a system and dangers must be designed out of it" [6, p.4]. The importance of "the right level of automation" can be nicely illustrated e.g. in the road transportation domain. There automated vehicles (AVs) promise to reduce the number of accidents caused by driver errors and enhancement of the transport efficiency [8]. Nowadays, modern vehicles offer automated driver-assistance systems for e.g. lane-keeping and blind-spot warning. These systems have the power to intervene in a safety-critical way. One of the design challenges is to determine what control actions have to be taken and when. A lane keeping assistance system should select an appropriate level of counterforce when reminding drivers not to leave the lane. While too much counterforce might hinder drivers (e.g. to do an evasive

B. Sangchoolie et al. (Eds.): EDCC 2024 Workshops, CCIS 2078, pp. 14–21, 2024.
https://doi.org/10.1007/978-3-031-56776-6_2

maneuver, especially when they are unfamiliar with the system), applying not enough force might not be noticed (e.g. when there are strong winds).

In this paper, we outline our vision of an approach that supports the early design of human-centered automation systems. We analyze the level of permissible interference scenario-wise by varying what control actions the automation can choose and when. We then determine whether applying these control actions in the given circumstances suffice to achieve the mission goal. To this end, we define for each variant a reactive game [17,25] of the automation system interfacing with the user. The control strategies synthesized for this game accomplish the control objective. Since they also take the human reactions into account, they implement the *shared control paradigm* [24] creating a synergistic control in which both the human and the automation contribute to the task. Our approach considers the impact of the automation's control on the human by using psychological models of the human mind. Since trying to capture human's mind necessarily results in a coarse approximation, the presented approach gives guidance rather than an implementable control strategy.

We describe the approach to determine the level of automation for shared control in Sect. 2. At the core of our methodology is a comprehensive understanding of human behavior. We achieve this by modeling based on cognitive architectures, which is described in Sect. 3. Examining the landscape of existing models reveals valuable insights into their individual strengths and limitations. A single architecture is not capable of capturing a broad spectrum of human behavioral aspects. To refine our understanding, we propose to integrate a combination of different human models. We conclude in Sect. 4.

2   Determining the Level of Power

To mitigate potential hazardous situations, an AV can usually apply a spectrum of responses, from activating an audible alarm to applying the brakes. Our approach determines whether a design variant can successfully adapt its control to the human and the current situation so that the operational requirements are met without hindering the human. Thereby, the approach can help designers choose between the variants that apply different level of control.

Control Synthesis. To implement the shared control paradigm, our approach uses control synthesis in a timed game between the automation system and the user. The strategy for controlling the automation system is synthesized while the actions of the human and those of the environment are uncontrollable. In this way, the human is not hindered and the synthesized controller implements shared control. A successfully synthesized strategy guarantees that the controllable actions are applied in such a way that the control objective is achieved, even in an uncooperative environment with maximum interference. This interference is modelled by introducing uncontrollable actions that formalize all possible forms of interfering. Therefore, the control objectives of automation system are captured as winning conditions of the game. For now, we will use winning conditions that can be expressed in terms of sets of states that are either desirable or undesirable. The reachability synthesis problem is hence important. It is about identifying a maximal subset of states and transitions in the game graph that lead into the desired states and/or avoid undesired states [17,20]. The latter corresponds to the safety control problem, where the goal is to consistently avoid a set of predefined undesired states. In a controllable game, the current state is within the set of winning states for the control player. Various algorithms to compute the set of winning states under different winning conditions are discussed in [17]. These computations yield an explicit winning strategy alongside. The problem of control synthesis can thus be reduced to computation of a winning strategy for the control player.

On the Need for a Human Model. To determine what control actions the controller should take when, we must model their impacts on the human and the technical system within their environment. While the impact on the technical system is a well-studied problem, our work focuses on the impact on the human. This aspect is currently less explored in the existing literature [15]. Our research therefore aims to fill this gap by providing specific considerations related to humans in the design of automation. We aim to explore the intricate joint dynamics of humans and automation systems in interaction through formal modelling. The objective is to determine the degree of automation, delineating the actions undertaken by the controller. The analysis is envisioned to be performed during the system design phase to facilitate the derivation of HCPS specifications. Moving along the levels of automation thoughtfully relies on a comprehensive understanding of human behavior. The inclusion of a human model becomes imperative. We use cognitive architectures as sources of human behavior models. Such models let us predict human behavior, thereby specifying what uncontrollable actions our controller has to face.

Formal Model of Human Behavior. Our approach necessitates obtaining a formalization that is amenable to game-based reactive synthesis. The construction presented by [13,14] manually translates an approximation of ACT-R cognitive model (cf. Sect. 3 for ACT-R) into a network of timed automata. To streamline the integration and translation process, we propose using model learning methods like Angluin's L* algorithm [3]. We adopt the concept of behavior from discrete-event systems [7], where the behavior is described by a temporally ordered sequence of events. Accordingly, the behavior of a dynamic system can be described as a language. Finite automata and their (ω-)regular languages are one of the convenient candidates to specify the dynamic systems. An automatic translation of arbitrary computational models into such an automata-theoretic modelling framework can be achieved by automata-learning algorithms, which provide mechanisms to derive finite automata approximating the target language with a specified degree of accuracy from finite samples. We propose using cognitive architectures as source for our human model. Moreover, we propose integrating the behavior of different psychological models of humans within a human model, *HM*. As illustrated in Fig. 1, various models are simulated using an identical scenario. The generated traces are then fed into a learning algorithm, in order to integrate them into one comprehensive and automata-based

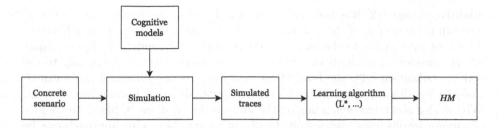

Fig. 1. Framework to learn a model of human *HM*.

human model. To enhance model learning and avoid over-fitting, we incorporate a fleet of different human models. Each model represents slight variations resulting from distinct valuation of adjustable parameters or alterations within the distributions of noisy selections. This approach enables the *HM* to capture a spectrum of possible behaviors.

Adapting Automation. The overall framework for adapting the power of automation is illustrated in Fig. 2. It describes a process that runs through a list of design variants and evaluates whether the current variant can achieve the control objective by applying its specific level of the power. On the far left, the game graph is represented that describes the HCPS. It is composed of the learned human model *HM* (including the environment) whose actions are uncontrollable, and the models of CPS components, whose actions are controllable. This game graph and the winning condition of the game, which captures the control objectives of the automation, are examined to see if it is possible to synthesize a winning strategy for the automation. If this is possible, the synthesis algorithm generates a winning strategy. However, if controlling the game is infeasible, the process ensues to update the set of control actions. The iteration process stops if either a winning strategy can be synthesized or if the last variant of control actions has been explored. If a winning strategy could be synthesized an

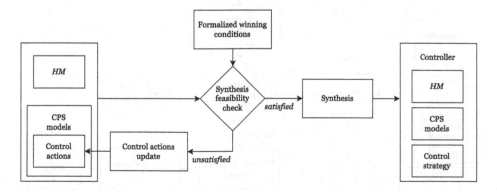

Fig. 2. Framework to design interactive controller.

adaptive design [12] has been achieved, which takes the human into account. The adaptive nature of the generated strategies makes it possible to adjust the degree of automation to the human and environmental conditions. For example, let us consider automation variants in the automotive sector. According to the SAE classification [22], the level of automation can range from 0 (no automation) to 5 (full automation). Each level represents different human involvement. Within this spectrum depending on the automation systems in place, the degree of human involvement varies from *hands-on* to *mind-off*. Our approach can be employed to determine when what level of automation is appropriate.

One shortcoming of the approach as described so far is that the feasibility check of the control synthesis may yield unsound results due to incompleteness of the learned *HM*. Since the *HM* is trained using a finite number of observed traces, *HM* might not reflect the original cognitive models sufficiently well. We hence co-simulate the CPS with the synthesized control strategy CS_i and the cognitive model in order to refine the learned HM_i (see Fig. 3) and subsequently to eliminate insufficient control. Therefore, the traces of the simulation that violate the control objectives are fed into the automaton learning algorithm to refine the HM_i. The result is a new learned human model, HM_{i+1}. After learning HM_{i+1}, we proceed the control synthesis following Fig. 2 yielding a new control strategy CS_{i+1}. As HM_{i+1} has been derived from the observed traces of a CPS controlled by CS_i, CS_{i+1} main purpose is to deal with the newly discovered behaviors. Thereby our approach realizes a divide a conquer approach of the control synthesis. Within the current framework, there is no guarantee that the refinement process will be terminated. Therefore, a termination criterion needs to be defined, e.g. when the synthesized controller has sufficient performance. The development of termination conditions is part of our future work. Additionally, by collecting real-world data, the generated behavior of the learned *HM* can be

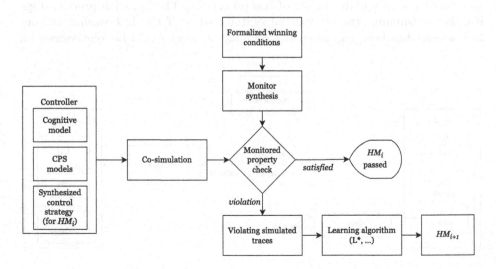

Fig. 3. Framework to refine the learned human model *HM*.

tuned by adjusting its parameters to improve its accuracy and adaptability to human behavior.

3 Cognitive Modeling

Cognitive architectures encode dynamic models of cognition based on established theories about the structure of mind [2,18]. Empirically validated, these architectures constitute plausible cognitive theories that enable predictions about imminent human behavior. Above that, emotions have a significant impact on decisions and influence individuals' daily choices [5]. Various configuration parameters affect the overall behavior of the cognitive model, such as the learning rate, the decay rate of memory, the retrieval threshold, and the noise distribution of knowledge selection, to name but a few. In the following, we briefly survey the research landscape of human models.

ACT-R [1] is a neurally plausible architecture with interconnected modules through buffers and a central production-pattern matching module. The input/output system consists of visual, auditory, and motor modules. The declarative and procedural modules constitute the central cognitive component by storing knowledge. The goal and imaginal modules track the agent's intentions and the internal representation of the world.

CASCaS [9,16] is designed for real-time simulation of human behavior in traffic scenarios. It has been validated extensively in aviation and automotive application, e.g. by [19,28,29]. It includes perception and motor modules as well as memory module for storing declarative (e.g., current speed limit) and procedural (e.g. driving instructions) knowledge. The memory incorporates processes for retrieval and forgetting.

SEEV [26] designed for predicting pilot attention, has been applied to predict driver attention in road traffic, e.g. by [4,10,27]. Modifying the SEEV parameters (*S*alience, *E*ffort, *E*xpectancy and *V*alue) leads to human modes, e.g. anxious, calm or bored.

There are a few cognitive architectures that capture the interplay of emotions and behavior as reviewed by [21], such as e.g. MAMID [11] and SAMPLE [30]. Cognitive appraisal theory [23] focuses on the processing of input stimuli to infer emotional states by taking the individual history, personality and current affective state into account.

4 Conclusion

This paper presents our vision on how to determine an appropriate level of automation in a human-centered system in the early phase of system design. The proposed approach aims to support designers to evaluate the automation variants in a structured way to choose the variants that guarantee safety objectives while realizing the shared control paradigm. Therefore, we propose to derive a human model *HM* from cognitive architectures using automata learning methods. The *HM* encodes human limitations and changing behavior patterns and is used in a game-theoretic analysis. The appropriateness of the level of automation is determined by testing whether a control strategy can be synthesized that implements the shared control paradigm and establishes the control objectives.

Acknowledgments. This research is partially funded by the German Federal Ministry of Education and Research (BMBF) within the projects "ASIMOV" and "TRANSACT", and by Universität Oldenburg within RTG SEAS.

References

1. Anderson, J.R., Bothell, D., Byrne, M.D., Douglass, S., Lebiere, C., Qin, Y.: An integrated theory of the mind. Psychol. Rev. **111**(4), 1036–60 (2004)
2. Anderson, J.R., Lebiere, C.: The atomic components of thought. Psychol. Press (1998). https://doi.org/10.4324/9781315805696
3. Angluin, D.: Learning regular sets from queries and counterexamples. Inf. Comput. **75**(2), 87–106 (1987). https://doi.org/10.1016/0890-5401(87)90052-6
4. Bairy, A., Fränzle, M.: Optimal explanation generation using attention distribution model. Hum. Interact. Emerg. Technol. (IHIET-AI 2023): Artif. Intell. Future Appl. **70**(70) (2023). https://doi.org/10.54941/ahfe1002928
5. Bechara, A., Damasio, H., Damasio, A.: Emotion, decision making and the orbitofrontal cortex. Cerebral cortex (New York, N.Y. : 1991) **10**, 295–307 (2000). https://doi.org/10.1093/cercor/10.3.295
6. Bowen, J., Stavridou, V.: Safety-critical systems, formal methods and standards. Softw. Eng. J. **8**, 189–209 (1993). https://doi.org/10.1049/sej.1993.0025
7. Cassandras, C.G., Lafortune, S.: Introduction to Discrete Event Systems. Springer, Cham (2008). https://doi.org/10.1007/978-0-387-68612-7
8. ERTRAC Working Group: Connected automated driving roadmap (2019)
9. Frische, F., Osterloh, J.P., Lüdtke, A.: Simulating visual attention allocation of pilots in an advanced cockpit environment. In: Selected Papers and Presentations Presented at MODSIM World 2010 Conference Expo, pp. 713–721. MODSIM World Conference, Hampton, VA, USA (2011)
10. Horrey, W.J., Wickens, C.D., Consalus, K.P.: Modeling drivers' visual attention allocation while interacting with in-vehicle technologies. J. Exp. Psychol. Appl. **12**(2), 67–78 (2006). https://doi.org/10.1037/1076-898X.12.2.67
11. Hudlicka, E.: This time with feeling: integrated model of trait and state effects on cognition and behavior. Appl. Artif. Intell. **16**, 1–31 (2002). https://doi.org/10.1080/08339510290030417
12. Landau, I.D., Lozano, R., M'Saad, M., Karimi, A.: Adaptive Control: Algorithms, Analysis and Applications. Springer Science & Business Media, Cham (2011). https://doi.org/10.1007/978-0-85729-664-1
13. Langenfeld, V., Westphal, B., Albrecht, R., Podelski, A.: But does it really do that? Using formal analysis to ensure desirable ACT-R model behaviour. In: Cognitive Science (2018)
14. Langenfeld, V., Westphal, B., Podelski, A.: On formal verification of ACT-R architectures and models. In: CogSci, pp. 618–624 (2019)
15. Lee, J.D., See, K.A.: Trust in automation: designing for appropriate reliance. Hum. Factors **46**(1), 50–80 (2004). https://doi.org/10.1518/hfes.46.1.50_30392
16. Lüdtke, A., Osterloh, J.P., Frische, F.: Multi-criteria evaluation of aircraft cockpit systems by model-based simulation of pilot performance. In: Embedded Real Time Software and Systems (ERTS2012). ERTS, Toulouse, France (2012)

17. Maler, O., Pnueli, A., Sifakis, J.: On the synthesis of discrete controllers for timed systems. In: Mayr, E.W., Puech, C. (eds.) STACS 95. Lecture Notes in Computer Science, vol. 900, pp. 229–242. Springer, Berlin, Heidelberg (1995). https://doi.org/10.1007/3-540-59042-0_76

18. Newell, A.: Unified Theories of Cognition. Harvard University Press, USA (1990)

19. Osterloh, J.P., Rieger, J.W., Lüdtke, A.: Modelling workload of a virtual driver. In: Proceedings of the 15th International Conference on Cognitive Modeling. ICCM, Warwick, UK (2017)

20. Pnueli, A., Rosner, R.: On the synthesis of a reactive module. Automata Lang. Program. **372**, 179–190 (1989). https://doi.org/10.1145/75277.75293

21. Rakow, A., Hajnorouzi, M., Bairy, A.: What to tell when? - Information provision as a game. Electron. Proc. Theor. Comput. Sci. **395**, 1–9 (2023). https://doi.org/10.4204/eptcs.395.1

22. SAE International: J3016: Taxonomy and Definitions for Terms Related to Driving Automation Systems for On-Road Motor Vehicles (2021)

23. Scherer, K.R., Schorr, A., Johnstone, T.: Appraisal Processes in Emotion: Theory, Methods, Research. Oxford University Press, Oxford (2001)

24. Sheridan, T.B., Verplank, W.L., Brooks, T.: Human and computer control of undersea teleoperators. In: NASA. Ames Res. Center The 14th Ann. Conf. on Manual Control (1978)

25. Thomas, W.: On the synthesis of strategies in infinite games. In: Mayr, E.W., Puech, C. (eds.) STACS 95, 12th Annual Symposium on Theoretical Aspects of Computer Science, Munich, Germany, March 2–4, 1995, Proceedings. Lecture Notes in Computer Science, vol. 900, pp. 1–13. Springer, Cham (1995). https://doi.org/10.1007/3-540-59042-0_57

26. Wickens, C., Helleberg, J., Goh, J., Xu, X., Horrey, W.: Pilot task management: testing an attentional expected value model of visual scanning. Savoy, IL, UIUC Institute of Aviation Technical Report (2001)

27. Wortelen, B.: Das Adaptive-Information-Expectancy-Modell zur Aufmerksamkeitssimulation eines kognitiven Fahrermodells. Ph.D. thesis, Carl von Ossietzky Universität, Oldenburg, Germany (2014)

28. Wortelen, B., Baumann, M., Lüdtke, A.: Dynamic simulation and prediction of drivers' attention distribution. Transport. Res. F: Traffic Psychol. Behav. **21**, 278–294 (2013). https://doi.org/10.1016/j.trf.2013.09.019

29. Wortelen, B., Unni, A., Rieger, J.W., Lüdtke, A., Osterloh, J.P.: Monte Carlo methods for real-time driver workload estimation using a cognitive architecture. In: Klempous, R., Nikodem, J., Baranyi, P.Z. (eds.) Cognitive Infocommunications, Theory and Applications, pp. 25–48. Springer International Publishing, Cham, Switzerland (2019). https://doi.org/10.1007/978-3-319-95996-2_2

30. Zacharias, G.L., Miao, A.X., Illgen, C., Yara, J.M., Siouris, G.: SAMPLE: situation awareness model for pilot in-the-loop evaluation. In: Proceedings of the 1st Annual Conference on Situation Awareness in the Tactical Air Environment. Citeseer (1996)

A Physics-Based Fault Tolerance Mechanism for UAVs' Flight Controller

Diogo Costa, Anamta Khan$^{(\boxtimes)}$, Naghmeh Ivaki, and Henrique Madeira

University of Coimbra, CISUC, DEI, Coimbra, Portugal
diogobaptista@student.dei.uc.pt, {anamta,naghmeh,henrique}@dei.uc.pt

Abstract. Unmanned Aerial Vehicles (UAVs) are on the rise across a wide range of application domains like shipping and delivery, precise agriculture, geographic mapping, and search and rescue. Thus, ensuring UAVs' safe operations and reliable integration into civilian airspace is essential. These unmanned vehicles face various potential hazards and threats, such as software or hardware failures (e.g., GPS malfunctions), communication failures, and security attacks (e.g., GPS Spoofing), which can threaten mission completion and safety. Thus, implementing a fault-tolerant mechanism to improve the resilience of UAVs is crucial. This research aims to introduce a fault-tolerance mechanism employing a physics-based model that accurately estimates drone positions in the presence of hazardous conditions, particularly in the presence of GPS faults. The physics model that relies on Newton's Second Law of Motion, enables real-time and precise estimation of the drone's position in faulty conditions throughout a mission. Thus, the physics model's values can replace the erroneous GPS input values. The results obtained through our experiments, conducted using fault-injection techniques in a simulated environment, demonstrate the effectiveness of our physics-based fault-tolerant mechanism, particularly in mitigating GPS-related hazards.

Keywords: UAVs · Safety · GPS · Fault-Tolerance · Physics Model · Fault Injection

1 Introduction

Unmanned aerial vehicles (UAVs) are aircraft that can operate without a pilot on board, being controlled by either a ground station pilot or an autonomous system. UAVs have proven to be versatile in military situations and are increasingly becoming popular for civilian uses such as deliveries, disaster management, rescue operations, mapping, safety inspections, crop monitoring, monitoring natural

This work has been supported by Project "Agenda Mobilizadora Sines Nexus". ref. No. 7113, supported by the Recovery and Resilience Plan (PRR) and by the European Funds Next Generation EU, following Notice No. 02/C05-i01/2022, Component 5 - Capitalization and Business Innovation - Mobilizing Agendas for Business Innovation; and by FCT, I.P./MCTES through national funds (PIDDAC), within the scope of CISUC R&D Unit - UIDB/00326/2020 or project code UIDP/00326/2020.

B. Sangchoolie et al. (Eds.): EDCC 2024 Workshops, CCIS 2078, pp. 22–35, 2024.
https://doi.org/10.1007/978-3-031-56776-6_3

disasters, law enforcement, and visually inspecting structures [1]. The reasons for their growing popularity include their user-friendly nature, agility, precision, cost-effectiveness [2], and ability to handle tasks that might be risky or challenging for humans [3].

While their adaptable nature, the UAV software and hardware are susceptible to faults and failures [4]. In our previous study [5], we examined common faults in a UAV flight controller, explicitly focusing on the PX4 platform[1]. Leveraging the open-source nature of PX4 and utilizing GIT bug reports, we identified and categorized the prevalent faults (i.e., or failures that can be considered as faults from the perspective of the entire system). We then, in our next research [6], injected these identified faults, in particular GPS-related (as GPS is crucial for precise positioning and tracking of UAVs) issues (e.g., missing GPS signals or GPS spoofing), assessing their impact within the context of U-space - a European Unmanned Traffic Management system (UTM) [7].

In the context of U-space, each UAV is allocated a separation minima (i.e., the minimum distance that must be maintained between UAVs in order to ensure safe and efficient operations), which defines a protective bubble around each UAV at every position (or an airspace volume throughout the entire mission). Violation of this allocated safe zone may lead to collisions. Thus, in the context of U-space, we define failure as a violation of the separation minima, which serves as a safety metric for assessing the impact of introduced faults. The study demonstrated that specific GPS faults had a significant safety impact. Our next study [8] revealed the main reason behind that. Our findings indicated that the PX4's position estimator, namely the Extended Kalman Filter (EKF), effectively filters more minor faults, but its efficacy diminishes with more significant or prolonged faults.

To address this limitation of EKF, we introduced a machine learning-based fault tolerance mechanism in our recent study [9]. We developed a machine-learning model using openly available logs from PX4[2] users worldwide. The study also proposed a two-layered bubble concept, introducing the inner layer serving as an alert mechanism. When breached, the machine learning model is triggered to predict the next position as long as GPS faults are being identified. In this study [9], we also explored the Haversine formula [10], which is a widely applied mathematical formula used to calculate the shortest distance between two points on a sphere using their latitudes and longitudes. This formula can be expressed in trigonometric functions and solved using inverse Haversine or inverse sine functions. This formula is commonly applied in navigation and GIS (Geographic Information System) applications [11] as well as in the industry and by the research community [12]. However, our findings revealed that while this formula is effective for ground vehicles, it lacks accuracy for UAVs.

---

[1] https://px4.io/.
[2] https://review.px4.io/browse.

Hence, the main objective of this paper is to apply a physics model suitable for UAVs, which will function as a key element within our fault tolerance mechanism for UAVs' position estimation in the presence of hazards, such as GPS failures, and abnormal conditions including jamming or hijacking.

We defined and implemented the physics model into the source code of the PX4 flight controller, conducted a series of experiments within a simulation environment (i.e., Gazebo), and employed fault injection to assess the physics model's effectiveness in the presence of GPS-related issues. The results reveal the effectiveness of our approach in improving the operations of UAVs in abnormal conditions and increasing safety and reliability.

In subsequent research, the integration of the machine learning model from our previous study [9] with the physics model used in this study will be explored.

2   Related Work

For UAVs, several research studies have focused on developing different fault tolerance mechanisms for flight controllers' individual systems [4]. One notable study [13] proposed an attitude control method based on the L1 adaptive structure for quadrotor aircraft, enhancing the system's anti-interference and fault tolerance abilities. Another research work [14] presented a design scheme using tri-redundancy technology to ensure the reliability of the Flight Control System for UAVs, thereby improving the fault tolerance performance of the aircraft. Additionally, another study [15] introduced a robust fault tolerance mechanism for UAVs in global grid inspection, which utilized a control system based on dynamic simulation of the satellite communication network and robust fault tolerance with a stochastic delay uncertain network system. Furthermore, [16] developed a flight controller for automatic carrier landing for UAVs, integrating disturbance observer and fault-tolerant control to address external disturbance, structure fault, and actuator fault. The work presented in [17] designed a sliding mode disturbance observer-based adaptive dynamic inversion fault-tolerant controller for fixed-wing UAVs, aiming to enhance the fault tolerance and control performance of the aircraft. These studies collectively demonstrate various approaches to improving the fault tolerance and control performance of UAVs' flight controllers, providing a valuable foundation for the proposed physics-based fault tolerance mechanism in this paper.

Another work [18] proposes a fault-tolerance architecture for data fusion targeting sensors and software faults on a quadrotor UAV. The authors achieve this by using an updated version of the weighted average voter, which gives a weighted mean of values obtained from the redundant modules. The voter uses the concept of the soft threshold and the agreement indicator to determine the consistency of input pairs and calculates a single output value based on the weighted values of each module. The paper does not propose fault tolerance for any specific sensor but rather for the data fusion system.

A study [19], more focused on GPS, proposes a solution that tolerates failures in the aerodynamic model, INS, and GPS. They achieve this by proposing a federated Kalman filter-based navigation method that combines the information from the aerodynamic model, INS, and GPS to estimate the position angles and directional velocities of the UAV. The proposed method is tested through simulations, and the results show that it is capable of providing accurate estimates, even in the presence of failures in one or more than one component. This paper offers fault tolerance by predicting the angles and velocities, whereas our model can replace the GPS sensor and predict latitude, longitude, and altitude.

3   Proposed Fault Tolerance Mechanism

This section introduces the physics-based fault tolerance mechanism proposed in this paper. A fault tolerance solution typically comprises two key components: error detection and fault tolerance. In the following subsections, we explain these two components within our solution. As mentioned before, in this study, we consider GPS-related issues as the faults to be detected and tolerated from the perspective of U-space, aiming to avoid any violation of separation minima (i.e., which is considered as failure in this context, that potentially may result in collisions). This section also presents how the proposed solution is experimentally evaluated.

3.1   GPS Error Detection

Following the concept of Bubble in U-space, in this study, we propose an approach with two layers of Bubble (i.e., a static inner alert bubble and a dynamic outer safety bubble) as can be seen in Fig. 1. The concept of an inner bubble is presented to define the minimum safety required by each drone that would not be violated by the drone in normal conditions. Any violation of this boundary could potentially result in conflicts with other drones. Thus, an alert should be generated and sent to the pilot or UAV control system for possible threats.

The inner bubble has a static calculation, as can be seen in Formula 1. Here, D_d represents the dimensions of the drone, including the wingspan. D_s corresponds to the recommended safety distance provided by the manufacturer, while D_m denotes the maximum distance the drone can travel at its top speed between two tracking points, which is static throughout the mission but not static for all drones and all missions, that can be obtained by the specifications of the drone's mission. To determine the inner bubble size, we select the greater value between D_s and D_m and add it to D_d in the formula. This approach ensures that the appropriate distance is considered for the inner bubble calculation, accounting for both the manufacturer's safety recommendation and the drone's maximum travel distance.

$$Bubble_{inner} = D_d + max(D_s, D_m) \tag{1}$$

The dynamic outer safety Bubble presents the concept of dynamic separation minima in U-space. Here, we propose a possible formula for the outer bubble that considers the influential factors on the operation's safety that may change dynamically throughout a mission, such as airspeed. As shown in Formula 2, $S_a(t_n)$ represents the current Airspeed, $S_a(t_{n-1})$ represents the previous Airspeed, $D(t_{n-1})$ represents the last distance covered by the drone. Utilizing these parameters enables the computation of the anticipated distance to be covered at time t_n.

$$D(t_n) = D(t_{n-1}) * \frac{S_a(t_n)}{S_a(t_{n-1})} \tag{2}$$

The relative alteration in the anticipated distance covered (expressed as $D(t_n)/D(t_{n-1})$ -¿ $S_a(t_n)/S_a(t_{n-1})$), caused by the alteration in the Airspeed, allows us to compute the additional space allocation required for each drone beyond the inner bubble radius. It is crucial, however, to ensure that the inner bubble radius consistently remains the minimum value. Thus, we determine the relative change in airspeed at each moment ($S_a(t)$) compared to the default airspeed, which should be a non-zero value (S_a). Then, as shown in Formula 3, we multiply the maximum value between 1 and the relative change in the expected distance with the inner bubble radius ($Bubble_{inner} * Max(1, S_a(t)/S_a)$).

Finally, to calculate the radius of the outer bubble at time t, the result of the previous calculation is multiplied by R, representing the risk associated with flying in the given airspace conditions (encompassing all other factors that may influence the operation). Indeed, R is an outcome computed by multiple factors, encompassing current airspace density, weather conditions, communication quality, U-space surveillance performance, and the age of the drone. R should have a value equal to or higher than 1.

$$Bubble_{outer}(t) = R * (Bubble_{inner} * Max(1, \frac{S_a(t)}{S_a})) \tag{3}$$

In this study, to simplify the environmental conditions and concentrate solely on GPS failure, we did not change the airspeed or other factors within our controlled simulation environment. However, due to the use of random parameters by the simulators for environmental setup, we opted for a value greater than 1 for R (in this study, we used value 2.2), resulting in generating two bubbles with distinct sizes.

In practice, to detect GPS-erroneous outputs (i.e., faults that originate GPS errors), the quality of GPS output data is checked before being used by the flight controller's estimator (i.e., EKF). We use the inner bubble as a threshold to check the quality of data. If the difference between the previous position of the UAV and the current position provided by GPS is higher than the inner bubble's radius, we assume that GPS data is erroneous. Hence, the physics model is used to estimate the current position of the UAV. Notably, Outer Bubble violations are deemed the most critical metric, representing a pivotal indicator of safety for both the drone and its surroundings as defined by U-space.

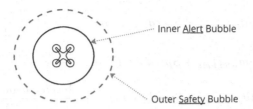

Fig. 1. Visualization of the two-layered bubble for fault detection.

3.2 Physics Model for UAV's Position Estimation

Drones are capable of three-dimensional movement along latitude (north-south), longitude (east-west), and altitude. The horizontal movements, along latitude and longitude, are achieved by adjusting the drone's velocity and orientation. For instance, the rotors on the north side should increase thrust to move north. The vertical movement, along altitude, is achieved by adjusting the thrust generated by all rotors or propellers.

Regardless of the direction of movement, Newton's Second Law of Motion remains applicable for determining the current position, velocity, and acceleration by considering the previous position. When dealing with UAVs, these calculations must be done in three dimensions: latitude, longitude, and altitude. It is important to highlight that GPS provides these coordinates in degrees, necessitating a conversion to meters before applying the law.

According to Newton's Second Law of Motion, it is necessary to multiply the speed by the time elapsed between measurements to know how much the traveled distance was and add it to the previous position, as in Eq. 4.

$$Position_{current} = Position_{previous} + Speed_{current} * Time \qquad (4)$$

This calculation is not enough because it is considering a uniform movement, which is a movement that always has the same speed. So, it is also necessary to calculate how the acceleration impacts the distance traveled by the UAV. The speed and the acceleration are correlated by Eq. 5, which states that the current speed equals the previous one plus acceleration times the time elapsed between measurements.

$$Speed_{current} = Speed_{previous} + Acceleration_{current} * Time \qquad (5)$$

By having the equation that correlates the speed and the acceleration and knowing that the speed is the derivative function of position concerning time, we can calculate the current latitude, longitude, and altitude based on the previous latitude, longitude, and altitude plus speed in the corresponding direction (i.e., V_x, V_y or V_z) times the time elapsed between measurements, plus the acceleration times the time elapsed between measurements squared, divided by two.

Formulas for the calculation of latitude, longitude, and altitude are respectively presented in Eq. 6, Eq. 7, and Eq. 8.

$$Lat_{current} = Lat_{previous} + Speed_Y * Time + \frac{Acceleration_Y * Time^2}{2} \quad (6)$$

$$Lon_{current} = Lon_{previous} + Speed_X * Time + \frac{Acceleration_X * Time^2}{2} \quad (7)$$

$$Alt_{current} = Alt_{previous} + Speed_Z * Time + \frac{Acceleration_Z * Time^2}{2} \quad (8)$$

Equations 6, 7, and 8 all follow the same logic, but each one is applied to a different axis. Latitude is the measurement of the position on the Y-axis, Longitude is the component of the position measured on the X-axis, and Altitude is measured on the Z-axis [20].

When operating a drone, it is important to consider the air resistance, wind gusts, and other factors that can affect its intended path. However, using the presented Physics Model, these factors are expertly managed through directional movement, resulting in more precise predictions of the drone's position. It is important to mention that the model's precision depends on how frequently the sensor values are updated.

3.3 Experimental Evaluation

We implemented the above formulas and the whole fault-tolerant mechanism within the source code of the PX4 flight controller. We then defined several experiments with fault injection to evaluate the effectiveness of the physics formulas.

Environment. In order to conduct our experiments, we used our evaluation platform, including a simulation environment created with Gazebo and PX4, which was also used and explained in detail in our previous studies [6,8]. This platform incorporates all the essential components required to execute fault injection campaigns, log flight data, and generate trajectories for multiple UAVs. All the platform components were developed, deployed, and operated within a virtualized environment using VMware ESXi.

Definition of Faults. In order to accurately test the physics model in various scenarios, it is important to simulate different types of faults or hazards that could occur in the GPS system. To achieve this, several failure conditions were considered. From these failure conditions, **three faults** were the most impactful ones have been selected for this study, as according to our previous studies [6,8], they had the highest impact on UAV's behavior. These faults include:

1. **GPS Failure:** which could also be caused by jamming or a hardware failure.
2. **Noise:** which represents noise in the GPS sensor or being in a crowded area.
3. **Random Values:** which could be caused by hijacking or radiation attack.

The injections were done at a strategic 90-second mark which lead the injection on turns or straight line, and the faults were injected for three durations: i.e., 5 s, 10 s, and 30 s.

Definition of the Metrics. To evaluate the impact and effectiveness of the physics model, we employ a set of five validation metrics. These metrics, previously utilized in our prior study detailed in [9], facilitate a comprehensive comparison between experiments conducted with and without physics models. The metrics include:

1. **Number of Inner Bubble Violations (IBV):** Instances where the drone violates the static alert bubble.
2. **Number of Outer Bubble Violations (OBV):** Instances where the drone violates the dynamic safety bubble, crucial for safety considerations.
3. **Flight Duration (s):** Measuring the total time the drone remains airborne in the given experiment.
4. **Distance Traveled (km):** Calculating the overall distance covered by the drone throughout the experimental period.
5. **Model Performance (m):** A holistic evaluation of the physics model's overall performance in all three directions: Lat Error, Lon Error, and Alt Error in meters. This metric represents the average of the error between the estimated and the original position.

Fig. 2. Flight plan for mission 1

Definition of the Missions. In this study, we defined **three missions** to represent real-world scenarios and analyze the impact of faults and physics models on drones when changing latitude, longitude, and altitude. The simulations took place over DEI, University of Coimbra, Portugal (i.e., the authors' department). The missions are detailed as follows:

1. **Altitude Variation:** As depicted in Fig. 2, this mission involves a shorter route with the drone changing altitude at each waypoint, ranging from 20 m to 50 m.
2. **Spiral Pattern:** Illustrated in Fig. 3, this mission features a longer and more intricate plan, maintaining a constant altitude of 20 m after takeoff and zigzag-style waypoints toward the end.

Fig. 3. Flight plan for mission 2

Fig. 4. Flight plan for mission 3

3. **Straight Lines at Higher Altitude:** As shown in Fig. 4 for this mission, designed to assess the model's performance in straight lines and at a constant higher altitude of 50 m.

Execution of the Experiments. We conducted three types of experiments to evaluate the physics model's impact and effectiveness: Gold runs, faulty runs without using the physics model, and faulty runs with the usage of the physics model. Gold runs are missions without any fault injection and provide a performance baseline. The faulty runs without the model represent missions with fault injection but no detection or mitigation, while faulty runs with the model use fault-tolerance mechanisms to detect and mitigate faults before causing significant damage.

4   Results

This section presents and analyzes the results obtained from our study conducted under both normal and faulty conditions, providing insights into the effectiveness of the Physics-based fault-tolerance mechanism proposed in this paper.

Table 1 summarizes the results obtained from Gold runs (i.e., fault-free experiments) and experiments involving three faulty scenarios (Noise, GPS failure,

Random Values), with and without physics-based fault tolerance (FT) mechanism, with injection durations of 5 s, 10 s, and 30 s. The table reports the average value of the metrics across three defined missions, including Inner Bubble Violations (IBV), Outer Bubble Violations (OBV), mission duration, distance covered, and errors in latitude, longitude, and altitude; the reason why we see the IBV and OBV as fractions in the table. The following paragraphs will provide a thorough analysis of these results.

Table 1. Metrics evaluation in Gold Run, Faulty Run with and without Physics-Based Fault Tolerance (FT)

Injection	Fault Type	#IBV	#OBV	Duration (s)	Distance (km)	Lat Err	Lon Err	Alt Err
0 s	Gold	0.00	0.00	213.50	0.72	1.66E-03	0.017	0.01
5 s	GPS Failure	17.67	2.00	212.76	0.72	1.75E-03	0.017	0.02
	GPS Failure with FT	0.67	0.00	212.29	0.72	1.75E-03	0.017	0.02
	Noise	1.00	1.33	214.40	0.72	1.73E-03	0.017	0.02
	Noise with FT	1.00	0.00	212.65	0.72	1.75E-03	0.017	0.02
	Random Value	6.67	2.33	218.14	0.72	1.54E-03	0.017	0.02
	Random Value with FT	1.00	0.00	213.10	0.72	1.74E-03	0.017	0.02
10 s	GPS Failure	29.67	11.67	222.30	0.75	1.75E-03	0.017	0.02
	GPS Failure with FT	1.00	0.00	213.49	0.72	1.75E-03	0.017	0.02
	Noise	38.33	10.67	214.92	0.73	1.74E-03	0.017	0.02
	Noise with FT	1.33	0.00	213.06	0.72	1.73E-03	0.017	0.02
	Random Value	11.00	9.33	214.50	0.74	1.73E-03	0.017	0.02
	Random Value with FT	0.67	0.00	214.87	0.72	1.72E-03	0.017	0.02
30 s	GPS Failure	51.00	18.33	168.57	0.29	1.73E-03	0.017	0.02
	GPS Failure with FT	1.00	0.00	214.62	0.72	1.73E-03	0.017	0.02
	Noise	40.00	14.67	219.32	0.76	1.75E-03	0.017	0.02
	Noise with FT	1.33	0.00	212.26	0.72	4.48E-04	0.017	0.01
	Random Value	39.67	13.00	222.29	0.79	1.75E-03	0.017	0.02
	Random Value with FT	2.00	0.00	212.62	0.72	1.74E-03	0.017	0.02

4.1 Safety and Violation Reduction

The reduction in Outer Bubble Violations (OBV) highlights the safety improvements observed in the study. With a substantial decrease from 250 to 0 violations or an average decrease from 83.33 to 0 across all missions, the model demonstrates a remarkable enhancement in safety. This reduction indicates a successful mitigation of separation minima violations, portraying a robust software-based fault tolerance. Simultaneously, Inner Bubble Violations (IBV) exhibit significant improvement, decreasing from a total of 705 to 30 or averaging from 235 to 10 across all missions. Importantly, these violations, although present, remained within the outer bubble, posing no safety risks but triggering alerts.

4.2 Distance Traveled and Flight Duration

Beyond the safety enhancements, the study's results showcase a notable improvement in the Distance Traveled and Flight Duration metrics. The application of the fault tolerance model yields an average distance and duration almost indistinguishable from the Gold run. Specifically, an average distance of 0.72 km and a duration of 213.50 s when the model is applied, compared to the Gold run with an average distance of 0.001 km and a duration of 0.71 s without the model. This parity in performance emphasizes the efficacy of the fault tolerance model in maintaining operational continuity.

It is also important to note that when GPS failure was injected for 30 s, none of the three missions were completed, and fail-safe was enabled in all cases. Thus, we observed low duration and distance covered. In contrast, when the model was being used in the same condition, not only were the missions completed, but also, no violations of the outer bubble occurred.

4.3   Position Prediction Accuracy

In terms of position prediction, the model demonstrated accuracy with low errors across latitude (0.017 m), longitude (0.001 m), and altitude (0.02 m). These errors signify the disparity between actual and predicted values throughout the mission. While the errors are minimal, ongoing monitoring and potential model refinements are essential for maintaining peak accuracy.

4.4   Visualizing Trajectories of Gold Run and Faulty Runs with and Without Model

Figure 5 provides an example visualization of the 3D UAV trajectories of mission 1 during a Faulty run (Random Noise) in mission 1 for 30 s, both with and without the fault tolerance model. The Gold run (Fig. 5-a) serves as a benchmark (or reference trajectory) for ideal circumstances, while Fig. 5-b shows the mission with fault without the model being used. Through the implementation of the proposed fault tolerance mechanism incorporation (Fig. 5-c), the UAV successfully completes the mission, closely mirroring the trajectory observed in the Gold run. This visual representation shows the practical efficacy of the fault tolerance model in navigating and adapting to unexpected scenarios, ensuring mission completion even in the face of faults.

4.5   Discussion

Analyzing the results underscores the pivotal role of fault tolerance and software-based resilience in ensuring safe and reliable UAV operations. The study aligns with broader research emphasizing the significance of fault-tolerant systems in UAVs to handle hardware and software failures [21–24]. The presented results showcase notable improvements in safety, distance traveled, and flight duration, emphasizing the critical need for integrating fault-tolerant control mechanisms and software-based resilience in UAV systems.

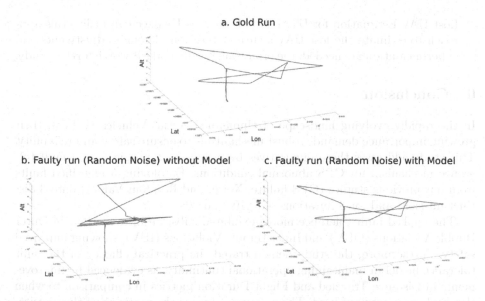

Fig. 5. Comparing Gold run with Faulty Runs (with Random Noise) in mission 1 for 30 s, with and without model

5 Threats to Validity and Opportunities

While the results of this study are promising, there are several limitations and threats to validity that could be explored as potential future directions for this research:

- Simulation Environment: This study was based on simulations, but it is crucial to test this mechanism on real drones in safe airspace. In future studies, it would be beneficial to test the model in real-world scenarios to evaluate its effectiveness in a practical setting.
- Missions: The study is currently restricted to a maximum of three missions, focusing exclusively on the simplified yet commonly used mission type. Moving forward, our intention is to broaden our scope by incorporating missions with diverse flight modes (e.g., Circle or Follow Me Mode). This will enable us to comprehensively assess the effectiveness and applicability of our fault-tolerant mechanism.
- Further Model Improvement: Although the formulas used in this study are effective, there is always room for improvement. Future studies could explore ways to improve the models' accuracy and efficiency.
- Multiple Drone Coordination: While this study focused on a single drone, future studies could investigate the effectiveness of the proposed mechanism in coordinating multiple drones in a collaborative setting integrated with U-space. This would be especially relevant for scenarios where multiple drones are required to complete a task.

– Lost UAV Estimation for UTM: UTMs such as U-space can utilize this approach to estimate the lost UAV's current position. Though adjustments and experimentation are needed, the promising results make it worth further study.

6   Conclusion

In the rapidly evolving landscape of Unmanned Aerial Vehicles (UAVs), their growing importance demands robust mechanisms to ensure safety and reliability. This study addresses these imperatives by proposing a physics-based fault tolerance mechanism for GPS abnormal conditions. Employing 3 identified faults from our previous studies (GPS failure, Noise, and Random Values) onto 3 distinct missions and for 3 durations of 5, 10, and 30 s.

The applied fault tolerance model exhibited substantial reductions in Outer Bubble Violations (OBV) and Inner Bubble Violations (IBV), showing improved safety. Furthermore, the study demonstrated the practical efficacy of the fault tolerance model in maintaining operational continuity, as evidenced by improvements in Distance Traveled and Flight Duration metrics in comparison to when the mechanism was not used. The outcomes showed the precision of the physics-based model in predicting UAV positions, with notably low errors in latitude, longitude, and altitude during execution. These findings contribute to the collective ongoing research, offering a foundation for further research and development aimed at enhancing the safety and reliability of unmanned aerial vehicle operations.

References

1. Joshi, D.: Drone technology uses and applications for commercial, industrial and military drones in 2020 and the future. https://www.businessinsider.com/drone-technology-uses-applications
2. Nex, F., Remondino, F.: UAV for 3D mapping applications: a review. Appl. Geomat. **6** (2014)
3. Jawhar, I., Mohamed, N., Al-Jaroodi, J., Agrawal, D.P., Zhang, S.: Communication and networking of UAV-based systems: classification and associated architectures. J. Netw. Comput. Appl. **84**, 93–108 (2017)
4. Fourlas, G.K., Karras, G.C.: A survey on fault diagnosis and fault-tolerant control methods for unmanned aerial vehicles. Machines **9**(9), 197 (2021). https://www.mdpi.com/2075-1702/9/9/197
5. Khan, A., Ferramosca, M.L., Ivaki, N., Madeira, H.: Classifying fault category and severity of UAV flight controllers' reported issues. In: 2022 6th International Conference on System Reliability and Safety (ICSRS), pp. 45–54 (2022)
6. Khan, A., Jiménez, C.A.C., Pablo, M.-P., Ivaki, N., Tejedor, J.V.B., Madeira, H.: Assessment of the impact of U-space faulty conditions on drones conflict rate. In: Trapp, M., Saglietti, F., Spisländer, M., Bitsch, F. (eds.) SAFECOMP 2022. LNCS, vol. 13414, pp. 237–251. Springer, Cham (2022). https://doi.org/10.1007/978-3-031-14835-4_16
7. Barrado, C., et al.: U-space concept of operations: a key enabler for opening airspace to emerging low-altitude operations. Aerospace **7**, 24 (2020). https://www.mdpi.com/2226-4310/7/3/24

8. Khan, A., Ivaki, N., Madeira, H.: Are UAVs' flight controller software reliable? In: 2022 IEEE 27th Pacific Rim International Symposium on Dependable Computing (PRDC), pp. 194–204 (2022)
9. Khan, A., Campos, J., Ivaki, N., Madeira, H.: A machine learning driven fault tolerance mechanism for UAVs' flight controller (2023). https://www.researchgate.net/publication/373757424_A_Machine_Learning_driven_Fault_Tolerance_Mechanism_for_UAVs'_Flight_Controller
10. Winarno, E., Hadikurniawati, W., Rosso, R.N.: Location based service for presence system using haversine method. In: 2017 International Conference on Innovative and Creative Information Technology (ICITech), pp. 1–4 (2017)
11. Python. geo-py 0.4. https://pypi.org/project/geo-py/
12. Wells, J.Z., Kumar, M.: Predicting sUAS conflicts in the national airspace with interacting multiple models and haversine-based conflict detection system. Front. Aerosp. Eng. **2** (2023). https://www.frontiersin.org/articles/10.3389/fpace.2023.1184094
13. Xie, K., Gong, Z., Bai, Y.: Dynamic trajectory tracking method of UAV using L1 adaptive control. J. Phys. Conf. Ser. **2252** (2022). https://api.semanticscholar.org/CorpusID:248413181
14. Zhang, C., Pan, J.H.: A study on fault tolerance technology of flight control computer for unmanned aerial vehicle. In: CECNet (2021). https://api.semanticscholar.org/CorpusID:245589507
15. Shen, J., et al.: Negotiation of the global grid inspection UAV with random delay uncertainty in an information communication network based on a robust fault tolerance mechanism. Front. Aerosp. Eng. (2023). https://api.semanticscholar.org/CorpusID:255600665
16. Xue, Y., Zhen, Z., Zhang, Z., Cao, T., Wan, T.: Automatic carrier landing for UAV based on integrated disturbance observer and fault-tolerant control. Aircr. Eng. Aerosp. Technol. (2023). https://api.semanticscholar.org/CorpusID:258980052
17. Dong, Z., Liu, K., Wang, S.: Sliding mode disturbance observer-based adaptive dynamic inversion fault-tolerant control for fixed-wing UAV. Drones (2022). https://api.semanticscholar.org/CorpusID:252860004
18. Hamadi, H., Lussier, B., Fantoni, I., Francis, C.: Data fusion fault tolerant strategy for a quadrotor UAV under sensors and software faults. ISA Trans. **129**, 520–539 (2022). https://www.sciencedirect.com/science/article/pii/S0019057822000131
19. Bao, S., Lai, J., Chen, Z., Lyu, P., Chen, W.: Aerodynamic model/INS/GPS failure-tolerant navigation method for multirotor UAVs based on federated Kalman filter. In: 2017 Chinese Automation Congress (CAC), pp. 1121–1125 (2017)
20. GISGeography. Latitude, longitude and coordinate system grids. https://gisgeography.com/latitude-longitude-coordinates/
21. Sadeghzadeh, I., Zhang, Y.: A review on fault-tolerant control for unmanned aerial vehicles (UAVs) (2011)
22. Puchalski, R., Giernacki, W.: UAV fault detection methods, state-of-the-art. Drones **6**(11) (2022). https://www.mdpi.com/2504-446X/6/11/330
23. Yu, Z., Zhang, Y., Jiang, B., Fu, J., Jin, Y.: A review on fault-tolerant cooperative control of multiple unmanned aerial vehicles. Chin. J. Aeronaut. **35**(1), 1–18 (2022). https://www.sciencedirect.com/science/article/pii/S1000936121001771
24. Nguyen, N.P., Xuan Mung, N., Ha, L.N.N.T., Hong, S.K.: Fault-tolerant control for hexacopter UAV using adaptive algorithm with severe faults. Aerospace **9**(6) (2022). https://www.mdpi.com/2226-4310/9/6/304

Defining an Effective Context for the Safe Operation of Autonomous Systems

Matt Osborne$^{(\boxtimes)}$ and Richard Hawkins

Assuring Autonomy International Programme, Department of Computer Science,
University of York, York YO10 5GH, UK
{matthew.osborne,richard.hawkins}@york.ac.uk
https://www.york.ac.uk/assuring-autonomy

Abstract. The safety of a system can only be demonstrated to have been achieved in a defined context. This is true whether it is a 'traditional' or autonomous system (AS). For traditional systems, a human is trusted to provide an oversight of operations, and react safely to unexpected scenarios that occur. For AS we cannot necessarily rely on human oversight to handle unexpected events, and must therefore be more confident that all possible hazardous scenarios are understood prior to operation. This makes the task of defining the context of safe operation (CSO) precisely and completely even more important for an AS so that unexpected scenarios can be limited. Attempting to define the CSO completely for an AS operating in a complex open-world environment could be an intractable task. It is therefore imperative that an effective and efficient way to define the CSO for AS can be found.

Existing approaches to defining the CSO for AS are generally seen to be disjoint (in that each of the elements is considered and specified in isolation) and lacking in focus (in that the level of detail is found to be inconsistent and often inappropriate). What is required therefore is a targeted, iterative and integrated approach for defining the CSO for an AS. We provide an example of how this approach can be used to deliver an effective CSO for an autonomous robot.

Keywords: Safety · Autonomous Systems · Safe Operation · Safe Context

1 Introduction

It is well understood that safety of any system can only be demonstrated within a defined scope of operation. A safety case for a system is therefore presented within an explicitly defined context. This context of safe operation (CSO) must also be defined for Autonomous Systems (AS). For 'traditional' systems, a human is trusted to provide an oversight of operations [11], and react safely to unexpected scenarios that occur. For AS we cannot necessarily rely on human oversight to handle unexpected events, and must therefore be more confident that all

This work is funded by the Assuring Autonomy International Programme.

possible hazardous scenarios are understood prior to operation. This makes the task of defining the CSO precisely and completely for an AS even more important so that unexpected scenarios can be limited. Attempting to define the CSO completely for an AS operating in a complex open-world environment could be an intractable task. It is therefore imperative that an effective and efficient way to define the CSO for AS can be found.

Defining the CSO for an AS requires an explicit description of what the AS is required to do, where it is required to do it, and how it should do it. This leads us to consider that the CSO for an AS must consider three distinct yet tightly coupled elements:

1. **The Operational Domain Model (ODM):** the elements with which the AS may be required to safely interact with whilst undertaking its tasks
2. **Autonomous Capabilities (AC):** the capabilities which the system is able to undertake in an autonomous manner.
3. **Operating Scenarios (OS):** the particular set of actions and events that the AS may undertake in order to achieve its objectives [5].

It is vital that all three of these elements are considered when defining the CSO for an AS since they all play a crucial role in determining the safe behaviour of the AS. It is only through understanding what the autonomy can do and where, when, and how that must be done (defined by the AC, ODM and OS respectively) that the hazards and hence the safety requirements for the AS can be determined. As such, it is the interaction between these elements of the CSO that should be the focus of AS safety analysis.

By way of an example, let us consider an autonomous passenger shuttle designed to ferry passengers between an airport terminal and car parks. If a safety analyst wishes to understand the safety impact of the failure of the shuttle's front-mounted LiDAR sensor, this can only be done with full knowledge of what the autonomous shuttle is going to do, the elements of the operating environment it will interact with in doing that (such as road infrastructure, other vehicles, people and weather conditions), and the scenarios that may arise as a result (negotiating junctions with other vehicles or negotiating pedestrian crossings). An analyst must also consider how the safe operation of the shuttle may be affected by changes in elements of the CSO during operation, such as the onset of heavy rain or wind. Understanding the inter-relationship between the different elements of the CSO is crucial. For example, decisions made regarding the scope of the ODM could affect the relevant operating scenarios. This may require trade-offs in terms of tasks performed and the scope of the operation which must be justified.

Ensuring the CSO is defined with the correct level of detail is crucial. It must be ensured that all the required information is available and that the specification is neither too sparse nor too full. If the level of detail is too sparse then we cannot be confident in any assertions of safe operation as we may not have identified all foreseeable interactions. Conversely if we require an analyst to consider every conceivable entity in a specific domain of operation we could end up with a state explosion of information without any clear understanding of each entity's importance or relevance. What is required therefore is a targeted approach that enables the CSO to be defined in a coherent manner that prevents a state explosion, and allows the analyst to identify and focus on the aspects most important to the safe operation of the AS (and not on the aspects which don't).

Existing approaches to defining the CSO for AS are generally seen to be disjoint (in that each of the elements is considered and specified in isolation) and lacking in focus (in that the level of detail is found to be inconsistent and often inappropriate). To ensure that the CSO for AS are defined in an effective manner, in this paper we therefore present an iterative approach which results in a more integrated and targeted CSO definition. We present this approach for review and posit it can deliver a CSO which can be justified to be sufficiently complete and correct.

The rest of the paper is structured as follows. We introduce our approach to a CSO for AS in Sect. 2, and consider how the AS can continue to operate safely in the presence of faults, failures, or adverse conditions in Sect. 3. We make concluding remarks in Sect. 4.

2   An Integrated, Iterative and Targeted Approach

Our approach, as illustrated in Fig. 1 (inspired by [1]), requires that the CSO is developed in an iterative manner. This helps to prevent a state explosion of information by ensuring that detail is added to the CSO only when its necessity is identified. As the spiral in Fig. 1 traverses the quadrants, the approach follows a cycle of design activities; updates to the CSO; safety analyses; and updates to the safety requirements. The final quadrant terminates by placing restrictions on the ODM in the form of a Reduced ODM (RODM). We return to the concept of a RODM once we have discussed the ODM itself.

In this iterative approach, design activities (such as selection of sensor technology, or architectural decisions taken) are the trigger to continue the spiral, and traverse the four quadrants again. A change to any element of the CSO will require a re-assessment of all other elements, and by continuously reassessing, and updating each element of the CSO throughout system development, the approach ensures a tight coupling between the different elements of the CSO to ensure it is developed in an integrated manner which increases in maturity with each design iteration.

Whilst we present the steps to iterate the CSO as the design matures, we are cognisant of the need to integrate the design lifecycle with the CSO. We aim to formalise this link as we mature the design and the CSO of an autonomous robot we are developing (see Sect. 2.5).

We next discuss the construction of each of the three elements of the CSO in turn, before going on to discuss how the CSO is elicited, developed, and matured.

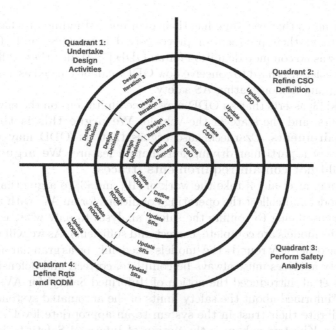

Fig. 1. The Iterative Approach to Defining the CSO

2.1   The Operational Domain Model

In this paper we focus primarily on the construct of an ODM. We do this for two reasons. Firstly, if not carefully managed, the ODM could manifest in a state explosion of data - the majority of which would have no material impact on safety. Secondly, the ODM represents the logical model on which the relationships of all elements of the CSO can be assessed as a point of reference.

The ODM must represent the variables in the environment with which the AS must safely interact with at run-time.

The current means by which the operational environment is defined and represented uses the example from the automotive industry which has started to consider how the operation of Autonomous Vehicles (AV) (or automated systems therein) can be safely assured through the use of ODDs, but there are many definitions of what constitutes an ODD for AVs. These include:

– The specific conditions under which a given driving automation system or feature thereof is designed to function, including, but not limited to, driving modes [13]
– Everything that an automotive system can be exposed to on the road [4]
– A subset of all the possible situations that could be dealt with by a human driver [10]
– A set of driving conditions under which a certain Automated Driving System (ADS) is designed to function [12]
– An abstraction of the operational context for an ADS [7]
– The domain over which an automated vehicle can operate safely [2].

Khastgir notes that everyone has their own understanding of what an ODD is, (either) to fit their products or preconceived notions [8], and Heyn et al. found there was no common definition for an ODD [7]. Whilst these differences in interpretion exist, it is hard to conceive how ODDs can be trusted as a mechanism for achieving and demonstrating AS safety.

Czarnecki [3] asserts that an ODD may place limitations on the environment, AS behaviours, and the state of the vehicle. **We argue this is the role of safety requirements.** Czarnecki also argues that the ODD may reflect the requirements of a particular driving automation feature. **We argue that an ODD should not contain requirements' traces.**

Gyllenhammar et al. [4] take the work of [10] and [3] to argue that an ODD is used to model and collect the operating conditions for an AV; with the ODD's primary purpose being to confine the safety analyses to only what is necessary (as long as the models are complete, correct and sufficient). As we will argue, this should be the other way round - the 'models' need only be as granular as required, but the safety analyses must always be complete, correct, and defensible.

Khastgir et al. introduced the notion of 'Informed Safety' for AVs [9] where drivers are "informed about the safety limits of the automated system to enable them to calibrate their trust in the system to an appropriate level". In a more recent article, Khastgir enhances the notion of Informed Safety to include the aspect of enabling a user to be aware of what a system can and cannot do (by understanding the conditions in which an AV is capable of operating safely) [8]. Khastgir defines an ODD as being the operating environment for which a system is designed for, and able to operate safely within (ibid).

We are aligned with Khastgir's definition of what constitutes an ODD, but because of the confusions and differing assertions that exist regarding the contents, and role of an ODD, we don't believe ODDs are sufficient for the CSO for AS. We have therefore established a simple, alternative, and distinct model which *builds on* the concept of an ODD, and which we propose for use with all types of AS, and for all levels of autonomy. This alternative model we refer to as the Operational Domain Model (ODM). The purpose of the ODM is to inform safety analyses. For clarity, we break down the ODM into its three constituent parts:

- **Operational:** The operating parameters (e.g. time and duration of operation) and any restrictions on AS operation
- **Domain:** The environment in which the AS will operate
- **Model:** The pictorial representation of the ODM.

Creating an ODM. An ODM is constituted by the Operational and Domain elements. The domain elements include generic elements (i.e. the meteorological environment and expected objects) and application-specific elements such as roads and drivable areas for an AV.

The operational aspects of the AS are kept as simple and as precise as possible, although we would always expect to see the 'Time Metric' (when the AS may operate), and a 'Duration Metric' (the permitted/required duration of operation). We may also expect to see elements such as 'Restrictions' (i.e. prohibited zones) placed on the AS in this part of the ODM. Such restrictions are not safety requirements per se (although they may unintentionally contribute to safety), but are imposed on the AS by the customer. Ordinarily, information regarding time, duration, and any restrictions will emanate from User Requirements in the first instance.

We identified two potential, yet opposite approaches for establishing the Domain element. Option 1 is not preferred as it requires the analyst to identify and classify every conceivable variable in the environment which could ever manifest. The second approach is a more pragmatic and balanced approach, and requires the analyst to provide only the minimum amount of detail **in the first instance**. To illustrate the contrast between the two approaches, we consider each option in turn.

Option 1 requires that **every conceivable object that may be present in the operating environment of the AS** is placed in a robust taxonomy which decomposes into entities, instances, dimensions, textures, and colours etc. The logical consequence of this approach is requirements for the AS to detect and classify each of these entities. This has implications on the selection of sensor technology, and for the data required to train and validate detection and classification algorithms. Such an approach presents two significant developmental risks - over-engineering the design solution (should specific capabilities not, in fact be required), and over-fitting the algorithmic training data [6].

As an example consider potential dynamic objects in the environment. Under Option 1, the analyst would need to further decompose these objects into biological and mechanical instances and then further by considering specific features, which for biological instances may include: Classification (animal/human); Dimensions (height, body type, age); Clothing (colours, and any headgear). When considering static objects such as permanent fixtures, the analyst would need to further decompose them by considering aspects including (but not limited to): Type of fixture (e.g. office furniture, or white goods); Dimensions; Uniformity of dimensions (i.e. is it a perfectly rectangular cabinet, or multi-castored office chair?); Colour; Texture; Opacity (i.e. a translucent, or an opaque door/wall).

Much of this data may not have a material impact on the safe design of the AS, nor its ability to safely operate, and following such an approach may not be commensurate with risk (as we simply do not know enough about the contribution to hazards at the early design phases).

Option 2 provides a more pragmatic approach insofar as the first draft of the 'Domain' element **contains only a high-level description of the dynamic and static objects** that are expected to be encountered by the AS. For example, for an office environment, this requires only an initial high-level overview:

- **Dynamic Objects** (biological/mechanical)
- **Static Objects** (furniture/building features such as walls, floors, or doors)

It is not yet necessary to model all potential variables of both dynamic and static objects (until further safety analyses are undertaken). For the initial representation of the **Domain** it is not (yet) possible to assert whether the AS should be able to classify objects - only that they should be detected (to maintain a safe separation). We can only identify any requirement to classify objects through analysis of the entire CSO.

It is only once we know the capability of the AS and its required operating tasks that we need to consider a more detailed model of the **Domain**, and any need to update the model will be identified through safety analysis performed against the CSO, as we will discuss later.

As an example of a generic domain model, for the environment, we would expect to see wave phenomena (aspects of the Electromagnetic Spectrum) and weather phenomena. Only the types of phenomena are considered at the initial stage, as their existence may not have a material impact on safe operation (and if it does, we don't yet know how).

2.2 Reduced Operational Domain Model (RODM)

Although AS are designed to operate 'within the ODM' it is inevitable that the AS will move 'outside' of the ODM as system and/or environmental variables manifest. The manifestation of these variables may make the operation of the AS unsafe immediately (in which case the AS may need to hand over to human control, or perform a minimum risk manoeuvre) - or may necessitate the application of restrictions on the operation of the AS.

Here we build on the work of Colwell et al. [2] and their proposal to establish a *Restricted* Operational Domain (ROD). The theory behind creating a ROD was to specify a domain within which a degraded automated driving system is still able to function safely (albeit at a reduced functionality).

A potential limitation of Colwell et al's use of a ROD is that it is limited to consider only how changes in system variables may place an AS in a ROD, whereas we have enhanced their work to also include consideration of environmental variables (both in isolation AND in conjunction with system variables). We refer to this concept as the *Reduced* Operational Domain *Model* (RODM).

As an AS design matures, and the elements of the CSO are assessed for potential impact on the safe operation of the AS (i.e. conducting a safety analysis of the CSO), system and environmental triggers which would place the AS as operating outside of the ODM are identified. Consider our robot which is required to transport small packages from A to B, and operate in all light levels. Safety analysis of the operating scenarios, autonomous capabilities, and system and environmental variables reveals combinations of variables which would trigger entry to an RODM, or make the operation unsafe. One aspect of these system variables relates to the AC of the AS.

2.3   Autonomous Capabilities

The AC describe the functions and tasks which the system can undertake autonomously. The automotive industry uses Levels of Autonomy [13] to define the overarching capabilities of vehicle types, but these are not a sufficiently granular means of defining the specific capabilities of an AS.

For defensible and compelling safety analyses to be undertaken, it is vital that the AC of the AS are accurately defined, and updated as the design is matured. For the initial draft of the AC, the analyst can only hope to define the required capabilities of the AS at a very high level of abstraction, but the level of detail will increase as the design matures, and trade-offs such as cost/benefit are decided on.

In their 2018 paper on informed safety, Khastgir et al. [9] argue that knowledge of the AC *and* the known limitations should be stated in order to develop trust in the system (which they define as a "history dependent attribute that an agent will help achieve an individual's goals in a situation characterised by uncertainty and vulnerability"). In the paper, they propose three levels of knowledge with which trust can be built. **Static Knowledge** is an understanding of the functionality of the AS. Whilst a driver/user of an AS could build on static knowledge over time (usage) we restrict the use of static knowledge to purely what is known from a design point of view. As the design matures, this should also include limitations (e.g. should there be a cost trade-off for a low-grade camera [9], safety analyses will be better informed with an understanding of any limitations in perception during periods of reduced visibility). **Real Time Knowledge** or dynamic knowledge about the automated system(s). Here we use the types of data that are intended to be fed to an operator/monitor (either human/machine/both) (and how), in order to better inform safety analyses. This should also include the means by which such data is provided. **Internal Mental Model** refers to prior beliefs influenced by external sources such as marketing material. Whilst this *could* be used to establish the trust in the system, it adds little value for informing the creation of an AC model.

Creating the Autonomous Capabilities. Restricting our efforts to represent Static and Real Time Knowledge, we can define the AC. In the initial AC model one might only instantiate the basic AC predicated on a Sense-Understand-Decide-Act model which states how the AS:

1. **Senses:** perform object identification; identify environmental variables
2. **Understands:** classify objects; perform localisation
3. **Decides:** conduct mission planning;motion planning
4. **Acts:** realise changes in speed and direction

2.4   Operating Scenarios

The current means to represent the OS differ between industries (i.e. the Concept of Operations (CONOPS) in aerospace and Use Cases/Operating Scenarios in the automotive industry, and we find no fault with these approaches. Our approach *builds upon* these approaches by introducing a graphical representation.

Creating the Operating Scenarios. OS are elicited as a specific instance of scenarios [14]. As OS are also conditional on the elements of an ODM, it can become increasingly complex to maintain the maturing OS in textual form - as can be seen for a single OS for an AS following a planned path in an office environment:

– AS is following planned path, and
  • Sender is in an inaccessible location, and/or
  • Lighting within building becomes too dark/bright, and/or
  • Doors are present between robot and destination, and/or
  • and so on...

As such, we have found Activity Diagrams (such as those described in [11]) a useful tool to manage this complexity.

2.5   Integrating the Different Elements of the CSO

In this section we illustrate the integration and development of the CSO by reference to autonomous robots being developed at our University. The use of bold font denotes the quadrant number shown in Fig. 1 as the process iterates.

The initial concept design (**quadrant 1**) specified the design intent for robots capable of delivering small packages around an office. The objective was for occupants to request a robot to come to them anywhere in the building and deliver a package to a desired destination.

As we moved to **quadrant 2**, we defined the initial version of the CSO. In the initial version of the AC Model, only a conceptual design existed, so we restricted our considerations to the generic autonomous functions of Sense, Understand, Decide, and Act, with processing distributed between these functions.

The initial OS was defined entirely based on the robot's Use Cases, Exception Cases, and Preconditions. For the ODM, the only relevant information for the operational element available to us related to restrictions (stairways and WCs would be prohibited areas), and duration (the robots would only be required for some duration during a typical working day). The domain element was initially limited to consider the variables that would constitute the office environment (zones, comprising rooms, corridors, stairs, and a lift; with rooms comprising walls, floors, and doors).

A Decision-Safety Analysis [11] was carried out in **quadrant 3** followed by a more detailed, yet targeted HAZOP analysis. The outputs from these analyses were used in **quadrant 4** to define an initial set of safety requirements predicated on maintaining a safe separation minima. The results of the HAZOP identified additional requirements on the detection of dynamic objects within a predetermined distance, and the ability to detect specific static objects which may present difficulties to available sensor technologies.

It was only possible to elicit meaningful safety requirements through the consideration of the CSO as a whole (i.e. the relationships between technological capability (AC), the objects in the environment and environmental conditions (ODM), and the tasks being performed by the AS at the specific instance in time (OS).

The safety analyses performed against all elements of the CSO also identified the system and environment variables that would trigger an exit from the ODM.

In making design decisions (selecting the sensors, operating system, and detection algorithms), we move to **quadrant 1** of another iteration of the spiral in Fig. 1. We are now able to update in **quadrant 2** the AC with the specifics of *how* the robot will sense, understand, decide, and act. We also updated the ODM to include the values for the light angles, brightness and temperature (which we had established through the detailed building design); along with the specific details of office furniture we had identified in quadrant 4 that it was revealed presented difficulties to the selected sensor technology in certain environmental conditions (a cardboard box, a 5-castor office chair, and a transparent container in this intance).

The selected sensor technologies were then tested for their ability to detect the static objects in the ODM (specifically those objects deemed to be 'difficult' to detect) as part of the safety analyses (**quadrant 3**). This was carried out under laboratory conditions for different variations of light-levels (including darkness), -temperatures, and -angles. In summary, we found that no single sensor was capable of detecting all three object types under all lighting conditions, and that the Point Cloud and the LiDAR represent the Minimum Equipment List (MEL) for static object detection when lighting is unavailable. This both derived safety requirements for the MEL (**quadrant 4**), and also identified the combinations of system and environmental variables which would place the robot outside the ODM should they manifest.

The identification of the system and environmental variables which would place the robot in a RODM then informed the need for a design decision for the acquisition of health and status monitoring solutions - and the spiral continued once more in to **quadrant 1**.

3   Monitoring the ODM

The ODM represents those variables that the AS will encounter and must be capable of safe interaction with, and whilst the system and environmental variables therein modelled are 'true' the AS is held to be operating 'inside the ODM' (and therefore operating safely). There will be occasions when environmental and/or system variables occur which place the AS 'outside of the ODM'. Excursions from the ODM may not necessarily be unsafe immediately, and it may be that the AS can continue to operate safely, albeit with some form of diminished capability.

3.1   Monitoring Domain Models

Colwell et al. [2] asserted the need to monitor ODDs and RODs and we are fully aligned with their approach. To assure the continued safe operation of an AS, we need to know when: The AS is operating inside the ODM; The AS is operating inside the RODM; The AS is operating unsafely.

To assure continued safe operation, we therefore need to identify the system and environmental variables which - either singularly or in combination - would place the AS outside of the ODM. This requires us to monitor identified variables of interest. Similarly, we also need to monitor for which values of variables will place the AS *back inside* the ODM.

The first step to elicit monitoring requirements is to identify the variables of interest to monitor. For example, whilst rainfall may be a causal factor in obscured sensors, or slippery surface conditions, it is the obscuring of sensors, or loss of friction which are the variables of interest for monitoring purposes, and not necessarily the causes thereof. Whilst readily-available, and reliable technology exists for detecting whether a sensor is obscured, and reliable technology also exists for monitoring friction, the same cannot yet be said for meteorological forecasting at exact location co-ordinates (as it may be already too late once precipitation has commenced). As such not only does identifying specific variables of interest prevent a state explosion (of monitoring) it may also lead to a simpler and more reliable solution to instantiate into a design.

So how do we systematically identify the system and/or environmental variables which require monitoring? Herein lies a benefit of having an understanding of all elements of the CSO. A systematic, deviation-based safety analysis of the CSO readily identifies whether a variable could detriment safety, and under which conditions. Treating each modelled element as a logical node, deviation-based analysis can be applied to the models. For example, a light level of 11 lx or under, in conjunction with a lighting failure could lead to an unsafe condition should there be a concurrent failure of the Infrared camera sensor; which would render the AS effectively 'blind'. This combination of failures/events may be unsafe when considering the operating scenario of the AS.

Assessment of the CSO elements allows the analyst to identify a set of variables which (either singularly, or in combination) will trigger an RODM. For light levels this could required three variables to be monitored: Light levels of the operating environment; Health (serviceability) of the Infrared Camera; and the Operational status of streetlights perhaps.

There is also a requirement for some secondary monitoring. As these triggers require the AS to moderate variables which it has direct control over (speed and/or direction), we need to be confident that the required action has indeed occurred (i.e. the AS has slowed down to a new maximum permissible speed for safe operation).

Any elicited safety requirements which place an AS inside a RODM/declare its operation unsafe *and* which also return an AS to safe operation, must consider levels of required hysteresis in order to prevent a repetitive cycle of moderating speed/direction as variables fluctuate. An example of this would be fast-moving clouds which may result in light-levels which change rapidly to values either side of 11 lx (thereby initiating a rapid alternating cycle of ODM - RODM - ODM - RODM as light levels alter).

4 Conclusion

In this paper we have proposed an iterative, integrated, and targeted approach for defining the CSO for an AS. The CSO is constituted by three tightly coupled elements: ODM (and the RODM), AC, and OS. We have described how these elements are developed using a cycle of design activities; updates to the CSO; safety analyses; and refinement of the safety requirements. This spiral of development of the CSO prevents a state explosion of information, and restricts the elements of the CSO to contain only those variables that matter to safety. We have also shown how these variables of interest are used to identify excursions into reduced and unsafe operation. Further iterations of the process are required before we can be confident in the effectiveness of our proposed approach through-life, however.

We are cognisant of the fact that we have only demonstrated our approach in a single application, so will perform further validation through application to other systems. We currently only model the CSO manually, so will look to explore more formal ways of modelling including the consideration of MBSE tools with robust ontologies.

We are also aware that our proposed process for the careful management of a CSO for AS will be dependent on effective integration with safety engineering practices, and acknowledge that this integration does not yet exist.

Current means for eliciting and managing the context of safe operation is not sufficient for the safety of AS. Despite the need for future work, we submit our approach for review and consideration as a potential solution to the shortfalls of current means.

References

1. Boehm, B.W.: A spiral model of software development and enhancement. Computer **21**(5), 61–72 (1988)
2. Colwell, I., Phan, B., Saleem, S., Salay, R., Czarnecki, K.: An automated vehicle safety concept based on runtime restriction of the operational design domain. In: 2018 IEEE Intelligent Vehicles Symposium (IV), pp. 1910–1917. IEEE (2018)
3. Czarnecki, K.: Operational design domain for automated driving systems. Taxonomy of Basic Terms, Waterloo Intelligent Systems Engineering (WISE) Lab, University of Waterloo, Canada (2018)
4. Gyllenhammar, M., et al.: Towards an operational design domain that supports the safety argumentation of an automated driving system. In: 10th European Congress on Embedded Real Time Systems (ERTS 2020) (2020)
5. Hawkins, R., Osborne, M., Parsons, M., Nicholson, M., McDermid, J., Habli, I.: Guidance on the safety assurance of autonomous systems in complex environments (SACE). arXiv preprint arXiv:2208.00853 (2022)

6. Hawkins, R., Paterson, C., Picardi, C., Jia, Y., Calinescu, R., Habli, I.: Guidance on the assurance of machine learning in autonomous systems (AMLAS). arXiv preprint arXiv:2102.01564 (2021)
7. Heyn, H.M., Subbiash, P., Linder, J., Knauss, E., Eriksson, O.: Setting AI in context: a case study on defining the context and operational design domain for automated driving. arXiv preprint arXiv:2201.11451 (2022)
8. Khastgir, S.: The curious case of operational design domain: what it is and is not? (2020). https://medium.com/@siddkhastgir/the-curious-case-of-operational-design-domain-what-it-is-and-is-not-e0180b92a3ae. Accessed 26 May 2022
9. Khastgir, S., Birrell, S., Dhadyalla, G., Jennings, P.: Calibrating trust through knowledge: introducing the concept of informed safety for automation in vehicles. Transp. Res. Part C Emerg. Technol. **96**, 290–303 (2018)
10. Koopman, P., Fratrik, F.: How many operational design domains, objects, and events? In: SafeAI@AAAI (2019)
11. Osborne, M., Hawkins, R., McDermid, J.: Analysing the safety of decision-making in autonomous systems. In: Trapp, M., Saglietti, F., Spisländer, M., Bitsch, F. (eds.) SAFECOMP 2022. LNCS, vol. 13414, pp. 3–16. Springer, Cham (2022). https://doi.org/10.1007/978-3-031-14835-4_1
12. Reddy, N., Farah, H., Huang, Y., Dekker, T., Van Arem, B.: Operational design domain requirements for improved performance of lane assistance systems: a field test study in The Netherlands. IEEE Open J. Intell. Transp. Syst. **1**, 237–252 (2020)
13. SAE: SAE J3016. Taxonomy and Definitions for Terms Related to Driving Automation Systems for On-Road Motor Vehicles (2018)
14. Ulbrich, S., Menzel, T., Reschka, A., Schuldt, F., Maurer, M.: Defining and substantiating the terms scene, situation, and scenario for automated driving. In: 2015 IEEE 18th International Conference on Intelligent Transportation Systems, pp. 982–988. IEEE (2015)

Towards Continuous Assurance Case Creation for ADS with the Evidential Tool Bus

Lev Sorokin[1(✉)], Radouane Bouchekir[1], Tewodros A. Beyene[1],
Brian Hsuan-Cheng Liao[2], and Adam Molin[2]

[1] fortiss GmbH, An-Institut Technische Universität München, Guerickestraße 25,
80805 München, Germany
{sorokin,bouchekir,beyene}@fortiss.org

[2] Denso Automotive Deutschland GmbH, Freisinger Street 21, 85386 Eching,
Germany
{h.liao,a.molin}@eu.denso.com

Abstract. An assurance case has become an integral component for the certification of safety-critical systems. While manually defining assurance case patterns can be not avoided, system-specific instantiations of assurance case patterns are both costly and time-consuming. It becomes especially complex to maintain an assurance case for a system when the requirements of the System-Under-Assurance change, or an assurance claim becomes invalid due to, e.g., degradation of a systems' component, as common when deploying learning-enabled components.

In this paper, we report on our preliminary experience leveraging the tool integration framework Evidential Tool Bus (**ETB**) for the construction and continuous maintenance of an assurance case from a predefined assurance case pattern. Specifically, we demonstrate the assurance process on an industrial Automated Valet Parking system from the automotive domain. We present the formalization of the provided assurance case pattern in the **ETB** processable logical specification language of workflows. Our findings, show that **ETB** is able to create and maintain evidence required for the construction of an assurance case.

Keywords: Assurance Case Maintenance · Safety Assurance · Tool Integration · Automated Driving

1 Introduction

Assurance cases are an integral component of the certification process of safety-critical systems. They are based on a goal-oriented paradigm, which places greater emphasis on explicitly stating safety claims, and supplying an argument along with assurance evidence that needs to be generated to support these claims [6,13]. In general, such structured arguments and evidence are captured in the

---

L. Sorokin, R. Bouchekir and T.A. Beyene–The authors contributed equally to this paper.

B. Sangchoolie et al. (Eds.): EDCC 2024 Workshops, CCIS 2078, pp. 49–61, 2024.
https://doi.org/10.1007/978-3-031-56776-6_5

form of safety cases, i.e., a comprehensive, defensible, and valid justification of the safety of a system for a given application in a defined operating environment.

The current practice of developing assurance cases is that safety engineers specify manually the arguments that connect higher-level safety claims to low-level assurance evidence. This practice of developing assurance cases is both highly expensive and labor-intensive, as it involves the extensive generation and meticulous maintenance of a substantial amount of evidence. In particular, assurance case development faces multiple challenges encompassing automation, tool integration, assurance distribution, and assurance maintenance. Although the manual definition of assurance case patterns may be unavoidable, the instantiation of system-specific assurance case patterns can be automated through the creation of automated assurance workflows. This automation not only reduces costs but also enhances efficiency by the automatic generation of assurance evidence. Tool integration presents another challenge, as diverse tools used in different phases of assurance case development must be integrated to generate assurance evidence. Yet, certification standards across various domains, such as DO-178C[1] in avionics and ISO 26262[2] in automotive, encourage the use of complementary tools when a single tool is not sufficient for a given test, analysis, or verification activity. The distribution of assurance across various stakeholders, system components, and platforms adds complexity, requiring careful management to ensure consistency and alignment with overarching assurance goals. In addition, continuous maintenance is required, particularly for systems powered by learning-enabled components (LECs), as updates to assurance artifacts, e.g., data and models, occur frequently. This necessitates an efficient maintenance procedure that monitors all claims and assurance evidence affected by these changes. Moreover, such a procedure should aim to minimize maintenance costs by selectively and incrementally updating only the portions of the assurance case impacted by these changes.

In this paper, we report on our experience in the development of an assurance case for an industrial Automated Valet Parking (AVP) system from the automotive domain. Our focus is on utilizing ETB[3] [9] to address the previously mentioned challenges. Specifically, the automation of evidence generation and claims maintenance. In that regard, we illustrate the steps involved in creating an assurance case for the AVP system. This encompasses the assurance case pattern creation, formalization of the predefined assurance patterns, and considerations related to assurance distribution and maintenance. Additionally, we highlight the lessons learned through our experience leveraging an automated tool-chain for assurance case generation.

The rest of the paper is structured as follows. Section 2 presents the AVP case study. In Sect. 3, we describe the assurance case development for the AVP system and the use of the framework ETB for assurance case generation. In Sect. 4 we discuss the lessons learned from our study and present in Sect. 5 related work. Finally, we provide concluding remarks and pointers to future work in Sect. 6

---

[1] Software Considerations in Airborne Systems and Equipment Certification.
[2] ISO 26262 Road vehicles Functional safety.
[3] https://git.fortiss.org/etb2/etb2.

2 The AVP Case Study

This section presents our AVP case study, which is based on an AVP System developed in the FOCETA project[4]. We use the AVP system to demonstrate the usage of ETB for the construction and maintenance of an assurance case.

System Description. The AVP System is a feature added to a car that allows to autonomously park the car in an empty parking spot [7]. In particular, the car is dropped off by the driver in a designated zone, where AVP takes over the car, computes the trajectory to a free parking spot and parks the vehicle in the spot.

The architecture of the system, which consists of several components, is shown in Fig. 1. We give a brief description of the components: The *Planning Component* (PC) calculates a feasible and collision-free path for the automated vehicle given the locations of the drop-off zone and a designated parking spot. The *Path Follower* (PF) controls

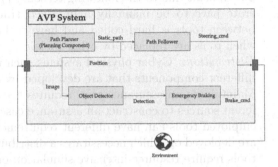

Fig. 1. Overview of the architecture of the automated valet parking system.

at every time stamp whether the vehicle follows a pre-calculated static path. During this operation, the *emergency brake* is triggered whenever there is an obstacle being recognized by the *Object Detector* (OD) within a safety distance from the vehicle. The path follower and the emergency brake together form the *Control Component* (CC) of the AVP system. To allow the save operation of AVP system, the following main safety requirement should be fulfilled [11]: *"REQ: The ego vehicle shall not collide with pedestrians, unless its velocity is zero."*.

Safety Assurance Challenges. However, maintaining an assurance case for AVP system, which claims that *REQ* is satisfied faces the following challenges:

(i) *Dynamic Assurance*: The AVP system contains a LEC, i.e. the OD component for the perception of other actors and objects. LECs are in general complex systems with large and multidimensional input spaces, whose correct behavior is difficult to be verified. In particular, it is not possible to know how these systems behave for any possible input when they are deployed on the street. Therefore, assuring the safety of a system whose decisions are based on LECs is complex. For that reason, a continuous engineering process is a common procedure in the automotive domain [5], where the system gets updated even after deployment, when for instance more operational data is collected to retrain the LEC model of the OD to improve the models' performance. However, when systems components are updated,

---

[4] https://www.foceta-project.eu/.

such as the OD, an updated assurance case has to be recreated. This recreation can be time and cost-intensive and requires a validation that all claims are considered for the assurance of *REQ*.

(ii) *Tool Integration:* Construction of an assurance case for AVP involves the usage of different tools, encompassing formalization tools [4], verification tools [1,2,15], or testing-related tools [3,20]. In particular, the certification standard ISO 26262 in automotive, encourages the use of complementary tools when a single tool is not sufficient for a given test, analysis, or verification activity. The correct orchestration of these tools is manually possible but difficult due to the following reasons: 1) artifacts which that tools generate have to be manually maintained/tracked, 2) the exchange of data between tools is hard coded and have to be reimplemented from scratch, when tools are replaced by other tools.

(iii) *Distribution*: Cyber-physical systems such as AVP are in general based on different components that are developed by distinct organizational entities. Maintaining an assurance case, requires the collection of evidence from different sources to construct an assurance case for the complete system. Also, employed tools can have different requirements on the infrastructure, they are deployed on which necessitates a distributed setup. For instance, testing tools require resource-intensive simulation environments, while verification tools may not.

Given theses challenges, an automated support for the continuous maintenance of the safety assurance throughout the lifecycle of AVP is important to save operational costs and guarantee that all envisioned claims have been collected.

3 Assurance Case Development Using ETB

In this section, we illustrate the development of the assurance case for the AVP system using the framework ETB. ETB is developed for the execution of distributed transactions and has been already applied to resolve the challenge of automating software certification workflows for the creation of assurance cases [9,17,19]. It enables an end-to-end, decentralized, and continuous safety assurance process where multiple entities are involved to establish safety claims supported by evidence. We outline how to use the framework ETB to establish the assurance case for the AVP system. Specifically, we commence by introducing our assurance case pattern developed for the AVP system. Then, we describe the formalization of the assurance case pattern in the language supported by ETB, followed by the tool integration. Finally, we sketch the distributed creation and incremental maintenance of assurance cases.

3.1 Assurance Pattern Creation

Let us consider a top-level assurance goal for the AVP system related to the safety requirement *REQ*. Although the primary goal here is not to develop a complete assurance case for the entire AVP system, in Fig. 2, we highlight three fragments

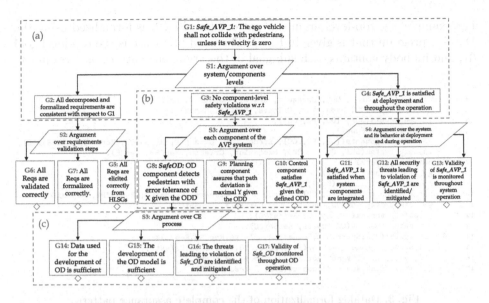

Fig. 2. Top-level of GSN-based pattern for safety case construction for AVP system.

of the argument pattern corresponding to various abstraction levels of the system with respect to the specified safety goal.

The first argument pattern, which is shown in GSN-like[5] notation in Fig. 2(a), divides the top-level goal, which is labeled as G_1, into three sub-goals, G_2, G_3 and G_4, where G_2 targets the validation of the input requirements, and, G_3 and G_4 target the safety of the individual components and the overall system, respectively. The second argument pattern is dedicated to composing assurance arguments from each component of the AVP system. As shown in Fig. 2(b), its three sub-goals, G_8, G_9 and G_{10}, target OD, PC, and CC of the AVP system. The third argument pattern, shown in Fig. 2(c), targets the OD component. Various recent approaches for the safety assurance of LECs propose safety assurance patterns over the LECs life-cycle [13,18,23]. Building on such approaches, our argument pattern for the OD component targets stages such as data assurance, model assurance, verification assurance, and run-time assurance. As shown in Fig. 2(c), its sub-goals, G_{14}, G_{15}, G_{16} and G_{17}, target design-time (data, model and verification) and run-time assurance methods and evidence for the OD component. The three argument patterns illustrate how assurance patterns can be constructed for the AVP system at different granularity levels by applying appropriate strategies.

3.2 Formalisation of Assurance Argument Patterns

As next, developed argument patterns should be specified as so called *workflows* and formalized in Datalog, which is the scripting language supported by ETB [8].

---

[5] In this work, we have only considered the Goal and Strategy elements as well as the Supported-By relation of GSN in our assurance case fragments.

For example, the top-level argument pattern (see Fig. 2) is formalized using the
Datalog program that is given in Fig. 3. The head predicate is the top-level goal
G_1, and its body contains each sub-goal of the argument pattern as a conjunct.

```
1   g1_safe_AVP(SUA, Reqs, ODD, Datasets, Specs, RepSafOD, RepSafPC,
2               RepSafCC, Scenarios, CrTests, RepCSM, RepME) :-
3       subcomponents(SUA, [OD, PC, CC]),
4       g2_reqs(Reqs, Specs),
5       g3_safe_components([OD, PC, CC], Specs, ODD, Datasets, RepSafOD, RepSafPC, RepSafCC),
6       g4_safe_system(SUA, Specs, ODD, Scenarios, CrTests, RepCSM, RepME).
7   g2_reqs(Reqs, Specs) :-
8       g6_req_validation(Reqs),
9       g7_req_formalisation(Reqs, Specs).
10  g3_safe_components([OD, PC, CC], Specs, ODD, Datasets, RepSafOD, RepSafPC, RepSafCC) :-
11      g8_safe_perception(OD, Specs, ODD, Datasets, RepSafOD),
12      g9_safe_planning(PC, Specs, RepSafPC),
13      g10_safe_steering(CC, Specs, RepSafCC).
14  g4_safe_system(SUA, Specs, ODD, Scenarios, CrTests, RepCSM, RepME):-
15      g11_scenario_based_testing(SUA, Specs, ODD, Scenarios, CrTests),
16      g12_cyber_security_monitoring(SUA, Specs, RepCSM),
17      g13_monitoring_and_enforcement(SUA, Specs, RepME).
```

Fig. 3. Datalog formalization of the complete assurance pattern.

Note, that the goal predicates in the Datalog rule contain all the variables
the goal depends on and a descriptive identifier, and not just a goal index like
the case for the assurance pattern. For instance, G_1 in the assurance pattern is
formalized as the following Datalog predicate:

```
g1_safe_AVP(SUA, Reqs, ODD, Datasets, Specs, RepoSafOD, RepoSafPC,
            RepoSafCC, Scenarios, CrTests, RepCSM, RepME)
```

In this predicate, the string `g1_safe_AVP` is a descriptive post-fix of the goal
name, and the parameters consist of the inputs such as `SUA`, `Reqs`, `ODD`, `Datasets`
as well as resulting evidence artefacts like `CrTests`, which is a set of considered to
be critical test cases identified by the system-level testing method. We illustrate
the description of the parameters used in the datalog formalization in Table 1.

3.3   Tool Integration

In this step, tools that provide evidence artefacts during the actual creation
of assurance case are integrated into ETB. Following the common practice in
tool integration frameworks, ETB provides a wrappers API that automatically
generates wrapper templates that can be customized by end-users for each
tool. As an illustration, the tool `OpenSBT`, designed for the search-based testing (SBT) of automated driving systems [20], is offered as a service through
the Datalog predicate `g11_scenario_based_testing(SUA, Specs, ODD, Scenarios`
`, CrTests)`. In this predicate, `Scenarios` and `CrTests` are artefacts generated by
`OpenSBT` and represent respectively failing test inputs and corresponding simulation traces, which contain positions, the velocity of actors over time.

Table 1. Description of the parameters used in the Datalog formalization. I refers to input variables, O refers to output variables.

Parameter	Description	I/O	Parameter	Description	I/O
SUA	System Under Assurance	I	RepSafPC	Report on safe PC	O
Reqs	Requirements	I	RepSafCC	Report on Safe CC	O
ODD	Operational Design Domain	I	Scenarios	Scenarios generated by system based testing	O
Datasets	Datasets used for training, testing, and validating OD	I	CrTests	Critical test cases generated by simulation-based testing	O
Specs	Formal specifications of Reqs	O	RepCSM	Report on cyber security monitoring	O
RepSafOD	Report on Safe OD	O	RepME	Report on AVP monitoring and enforcement	O

In ETB each tool can be evaluated under so-called one or more *modes*. A mode specifies which variables serve as input or output of the corresponding tool. For example, the mode used for the predicate g11_scenario_based_testing (SUA, Specs, ODD, Scenarios, CrTests) is (+,+,+,-,-). That means that the first input argument, which is the SUA, is of type string and holds the path to the system-under-assurance to be tested in the SBT tool, the second and third input arguments are files that capture the specifications and ODD constraints, while the two last arguments are files generated by OpenSBT. An example of a wrapper used to invoke OpenSBT is shown in Fig. 4.

```
1  public class OpenSBTWRP extends OpenSBTETBWRP {
2    @Override
3    public void run() {
4      if (mode.equals("+++--")) {
5        //1. Invoke OpenSBT
6        String suaPath = arg1;
7        File specs = new File(arg2);
8        File oddFile = new File(arg2);
9        String odd = getOddFromFile(oddFile);
10       String openSBT_CMD ="bash interface.sh "+ suaPath + " "+ specs + " "+ odd;
11       String openSBT_Outputs = this.runCMDO(openSBT_CMD);
12       //2. Evidence generation
13       String[] paths = openSBT_Outputs.split("\n");
14       String criticalTcFilePath = this.workSpaceDirPath+"CriticalTC";
15       this.createLocalFile(paths[0], criticalTcFilePath);
16       this.arg3 = criticalTcFilePath;
17       arg4 = new ArrayList<String>();
18       this.createLocalFiles(paths, arg4);
19       //Add claim to claimDB
20       this.addClaimPredicate();
21     }
22     ...
23  }
```

Fig. 4. Implementation of a wrapper for the integration of OpenSBT into ETB.

3.4 Distributed Assurance

The usage of ETB enables the creation of both assurance cases and evidence artefacts by executing the Datalog workflows in a distributed setting. Practically, a network of so called ETB nodes can be defined where each node can create assurance cases or evidence artefacts depending on the type of the workflow it contains. In particular, each entity that wants to contribute to the assurance case - by providing a tool - has to deploy an ETB node. When a workflow is given to an ETB node, it automatically identifies tools of other nodes which can contribute with their evidence to the overall assurance case.

As an example, consider the usage of a tool that helps to adapt the ODD at the runtime of the AVP system. In particular, this tool derives at runtime of AVP constraints from execution traces where the system behaves critically or not. Such tool can be for instance HyTeM [4]. The derived constraints, i.e., the updated ODD, serve as an input for the system-level-testing tool OpenSBT (s. described in the previous section). While OpenSBT, is a testing tool that needs a comprehensive simulation environment with high resource usage, HyTeM requires considerably less resources and can be deployed in a different environment. The collection of distributed evidence provided by HyTeM and OpenSBT can be managed by ETB by the deployment of two ETB nodes: where one ETB node provides evidence from OpenSBT, while another ETB node is deployed on a different platform.

3.5 Automated Safety Case Creation

ETB provides a top-down left-to-right Datalog engine that automatically executes the assurance workflow specified in Datalog. A datalog claim that can be instantiated, corresponds to an assurance claim with sufficient evidence. By the end of the execution of the assurance workflow, ETB returns either the list of claims, i.e., a complete assurance case or a counter-example that points to the failed step (sub-goal or tool execution) of the assurance workflow. The established claims, sub-claims, and evidence, which compose the assurance case for the AVP system, are given in Fig. 5. Figure 5 a) shows the claims in the database in ETB and Fig. 5 (b) shows the corresponding GSN of the safety case.

As visualized in Fig. 5(a), the created claims can be further categorized into two classes, namely *high-level claims* and *low-level claims*. While high-level claims correspond to the goals in the argument patterns that are supported by a set of sub-claims and a connecting argument, low-level claims are directly supported by evidence artifacts. For instance, the highlighted claim in green in Fig. 5(b) corresponding to the goal G_{11}, is supported by the evidence generated by OpenSBT, as depicted in Fig. 6. ETB stores all these claims in a claims table and keeps track of all relevant and integrated tools and workflows w.r.t a given claim.

3.6 Assurance Case Maintenance

One defining feature of the proposed process is continuous assurance case maintenance, where updates to the SUA, its requirements, or verification plans are

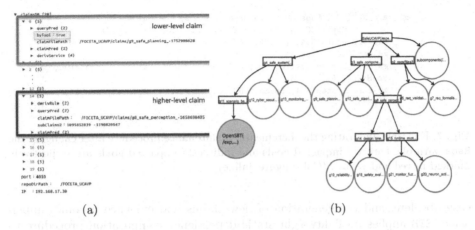

(a)   (b)

Fig. 5. a) shows an excerpt of the claim database of ETB in JSON format and b) shows an overview of corresponding claims in GSN-based format.

```
...  => query: openSBT(/experiments/PedestrianCrossing/Leuven_AVP_ori/Demo_AVP.pb, odd.txt-null,
       CriticalTc, Traces)++--
    -> no matching workflow
    -> [WARNING] processing via workflows not successful
            -> invoking a local service
            -> invoking a user service
    -> [claim] : openSBT(/experiments/PedestrianCrossing/Leuven_AVP_ori/Demo_AVP.pb, odd.txt-
       8eded3cc64b062d93303afdf97e6400b1e9159d0, claimFiles/openSBT_1924485658CriticalTC-
       2322744390fc63916ef12096e91797145ea8c809, [claimFiles/openSBT_1924485658/traces_1-
       315f778a226d8483224ecb5bb94922c0d6604ce0, claimFiles/openSBT_1924485658/traces_2-
       018afaa76b143846436f9852bdff85557b7ad5af, claimFiles/openSBT_1924485658/traces_3-
       315f778a226d8483224ecb5bb94922c0d6604ce0, claimFiles/openSBT_1924485658/traces_4-
       f1d3583b0d650b5564294330fa33086f02f85ee9, claimFiles/openSBT_1924485658/traces_5-
       315f778a226d8483224ecb5bb94922c0d6604ce0, claimFiles/openSBT_1924485658/traces_6-
       f8d4c22c0cb7591afc4b0253350cfde8afb7c491, claimFiles/openSBT_1924485658/traces_7-
       315f778a226d8483224ecb5bb94922c0d6604ce0, claimFiles/openSBT_1924485658/traces_8-
       f8d4c22c0cb7591afc4b0253350cfde8afb7c491, claimFiles/openSBT_1924485658/traces_9-
       f8d4c22c0cb7591afc4b0253350cfde8afb7c491, claimFiles/openSBT_1924485658/traces_10-
       b431b9a1e96c96dba5f5a96b229fe7c81a579686])++++
    -> [✓] claim added
```

Fig. 6. Console output of ETB after triggering OpenSBT. OpenSBT identifies critical test inputs with corresponding traces whose path is given on the right half of the Figure. These artefacts serve as evidence and are managed internally by ETB using a hash identifier as shown on the left part of the Figure.

anticipated. In the event of such updates, outdated assurance artefacts including assurance cases and evidence artefacts are incrementally maintained, i.e., only a minimal set of maintenance actions are identified and executed. The ETB framework enables such assurance process by continuously executing relevant Datalog programs for outdated assurance cases and by continuously invoking verification tools for outdated assurance artefacts.

Let us consider the top-level claim g1_safeAVP created for the AVP system. A common practice involves leveraging operational data to refine LECs, facilitating adjustments/improvements based on the evolving operational environment. Specifically, operational data plays a crucial role in refining the requirements and ODD [21]. Yet, any updates to the requirements render the existing safety

```
1   g1_safe_AVP(SUA, Reqs, ODD, Datasets, Specs,  RepSafOD, RepSafPC,
2               RepSafCC, ScenariosSBT, CrTests, RepCSM, RepME) :-
3       subcomponents(SUA, [OD, PC, CC]),
4       g2_reqs(Reqs, Specs),
5       g3_safe_components([OD, PC, CC], Specs, ODD, Datasets, RepSafOD,
        RepSafPC, RepSafCC),
6       g4_safe_system(SUA, Specs, ODD, ScenariosSBT, CrTests, RepCSM,
        RepME).
```

Fig. 7. Example illustrating the incremental maintenance procedure after changing the Reqs variable. Directly impacted goals and indirectly impacted goals are respectively marked in red and yellow. (Color figure online)

case obsolete, and the generation of new claims and evidence becomes imperative. ETB applies its lightweight static dependency computation procedure to compute a sub-tree of the assurance case impacted by such update. The procedure is applied to the formalized assurance pattern that was executed during the establishment of the top-level claim.

In particular, the maintenance procedure distinguishes between two types of goals: *directly impacted goals* and *indirectly impacted goals* (s. Fig. 7). Directly impacted goals, such as G_1, G_2, G_6 and G_7 are always re-run to re-establish their corresponding claims. However, indirectly impacted goals, which are G_3, G_4, G_8, G_9, and G_{10}, may not need re-running if the re-running of the directly impacted goals did not result in an update to their assurance artefact.

4   Discussion

In this section, we discuss on the experience of using the Evidential Tool Bus for assurance case maintenance and the limitations of ETB, when generating assurance cases for automated driving systems. The case study reveals that the ETB framework provides computer-aided support for developing assurance cases, where it enables the automated execution of assurance workflows, fostering scalability in assurance evidence generation and maintenance. Additionally, ETB facilitates the distributed execution of assurance workflows, along with the orchestration and integration of various tools utilized in evidence generation.

However, we note that the specification, and validation of these Datalog-based workflows have to be done manually by the user. From our experience, the concrete manual specification of assurance workflows is manageable for simple workflows, as Datalog is a declarative specification language with a simple syntax. However, a comprehensive assurance case may involve a significant number of nodes to cover further aspects of the system's functionality such as fault tolerance, and to provide a sufficient analysis. Further, in our example, we did not prove the validity of single claims, such as, e.g., how confident the system-level testing tool OpenSBT is that a test case is critical or that no further failing tests exist. However, confidence scores can be similarly incorporated into the workflow specification and modeled as an argument in a Datalog predicate of the corresponding tool.

5 Related Work

This section provides a brief overview on research works on assurance cases and dynamic assurance case maintenance [22]. Recently, there has been work on assurance case pattern selection [13,18], and assurance case pattern instantiation [10,14,16,23]. We focus on the latter one, as this is the main challenge considered in our paper.

Hawkins et al. [13] have presented a methodology for the instantiation of assurance cases for autonomous systems containing ML components. The methodology comprises a set of safety case patterns and a process for (1) systematically integrating safety assurance into the ML component life cycle, as well as (2) generating the evidence base for explicitly justifying the acceptable safety of integrated ML components. While AMLAS covers several stages of the ML life-cycle, computer-aided support to automate the assurance case construction as well as its maintenance in case of requirements or system changes, as supported by ETB, is not discussed. In contrast, a recent work [19] proposed to "automate" the evaluation of software assurance evidence to enable certifiers to determine rapidly that system risks are acceptable. They adopted a tool-based approach to the construction of software artifacts that are supported by rigorous evidence. This concept is very important, especially for certification, where it is desirable that arguments representing safety assurance can be re-playable.

Ramakrishna et al. [16] developed the tool ACG for the automated assurance case generation, given a manually curated evidence store. The evidence store is populated with evidence artifacts, which are automatically generated from the system model architecture. While ACG automatizes the safety case instantiation, it lacks a mechanism to support dynamic safety assurance as enabled by ETB. The toolset AdvoCATE [10] supports the development of assurance cases and has been applied to a use case for swift unmanned aircraft system but also here no assurance case maintenance is possible.

6 Conclusion

In this paper, we presented the utilization of the ETB framework as computer-aided support for the development of an assurance case for an automated driving system. We illustrated the formalization of the assurance case as a Datalog program and have shown the integration of a testing tool to provide evidence for the argumentation of the safety of the system at the system level. In addition, we outlined the distributed execution of tools integrated with ETB to cope with different levels of interoperability of tools and heterogeneity of providers, as well as described how the incremental assurance is supported by ETB.

In our future work, we plan to extend our study incorporating all tools required to instantiate a complete assurance case for the AVP system. Further, we are working on an approach that enables to generate ETB workflows, i.e., Datalog specifications, from assurance case patterns represented as GSN to facilitate the application of ETB for the assurance case creation. Furthermore, we plan to extend ETB to support a comprehensive confidence argumentation [12].

Acknowledgments

▨ This work is part of FOCETA project that has received funding from the European Union's Horizon 2020 research and innovation program under grant agreement N. 956123.

References

1. CppCheck. https://github.com/danmar/cppcheck
2. Infer. https://fbinfer.com/
3. Prescan. https://plm.sw.siemens.com/en-US/simcenter/autonomous-vehicle-solutions/prescan/
4. Bartocci, E., Mateis, C., Nesterini, E., Ničković, D.: Mining hyperproperties using temporal logics. ACM Trans. Embed. Comput. Syst. **22**(5s) (2023). https://doi.org/10.1145/3609394
5. Bensalem, S., et al.: Continuous engineering for trustworthy learning-enabled autonomous systems. In: Steffen, B. (ed.) Bridging the Gap Between AI and Reality, pp. 256–278. Springer Nature Switzerland, Cham (2024). https://doi.org/10.1007/978-3-031-46002-9_15
6. Bishop, P., Bloomfield, R.: A methodology for safety case development. In: Safety and Reliability, vol. 20, pp. 34–42. Taylor & Francis (2000)
7. Bosch: automated valet parking. https://www.bosch-mobility.com/de/loesungen/parken/automated-valet-parking/
8. Ceri, S., Gottlob, G., Tanca, L.: What you always wanted to know about datalog (and never dared to ask). IEEE Trans. Knowl. Data Eng. **1**, 146–166 (1989)
9. Cruanes, S., Hamon, G., Owre, S., Shankar, N.: Tool integration with the evidential tool bus. In: Giacobazzi, R., Berdine, J., Mastroeni, I. (eds.) VMCAI 2013. LNCS, vol. 7737, pp. 275–294. Springer, Heidelberg (2013). https://doi.org/10.1007/978-3-642-35873-9_18
10. Denney, E., Pai, G.: Tool support for assurance case development. Autom. Softw. Eng. **25**(3), 435–499 (2018)
11. Esen, H., Liao, B.H.C.: Simulation-based safety assurance for an AVP system incorporating learning-enabled components (2023)
12. Hawkins, R., Kelly, T., Knight, J., Graydon, P.: A new approach to creating clear safety arguments. In: Dale, C., Anderson, T. (eds.) Advances in Systems Safety, pp. 3–23. Springer, London (2011). https://doi.org/10.1007/978-0-85729-133-2_1
13. Hawkins, R., Paterson, C., Picardi, C., Jia, Y., Calinescu, R., Habli, I.: Guidance on the assurance of machine learning in autonomous systems (AMLAS) (2021)
14. Kaur, R., Ivanov, R., Cleaveland, M., Sokolsky, O., Lee, I.: Assurance case patterns for cyber-physical systems with deep neural networks. In: Casimiro, A., Ortmeier, F., Schoitsch, E., Bitsch, F., Ferreira, P. (eds.) SAFECOMP 2020. LNCS, vol. 12235, pp. 82–97. Springer, Cham (2020). https://doi.org/10.1007/978-3-030-55583-2_6
15. Liao, B.H., Cheng, C., Esen, H., Knoll, A.: Are transformers more robust? towards exact robustness verification for transformers. In: SAFECOMP 2023, vol. 14181, pp. 89–103 (2023)
16. Ramakrishna, S., Hartsell, C., Dubey, A., Pal, P.P., Karsai, G.: A methodology for automating assurance case generation. CoRR abs/2003.05388 (2020), https://arxiv.org/abs/2003.05388
17. Ruess, H., Shankar, N.: Evidential transactions with cyberlogic (2023)

18. Schwalbe, G., Knie, B., Sämann, T., Dobberphul, T., Gauerhof, L., Raafatnia, S., Rocco, V.: Structuring the safety argumentation for deep neural network based perception in automotive applications. In: Casimiro, A., Ortmeier, F., Schoitsch, E., Bitsch, F., Ferreira, P. (eds.) SAFECOMP 2020. LNCS, vol. 12235, pp. 383–394. Springer, Cham (2020). https://doi.org/10.1007/978-3-030-55583-2_29

19. Shankar, N., et al.: Descert: design for certification (2022)

20. Sorokin, L., Munaro, T., Safin, D., Liao, B.H.C., Molin, A.: OpenSBT: a modular framework for search-based testing of automated driving systems. In: Tool Demonstration Track ICSE 2024

21. Tonk, A., Boussif, A., Beugin, J., Collart-Dutilleul, S.: Towards a specified operational design domain for a safe remote driving of trains. In: Proceedings of the 31st European Safety and Reliability Conference, Angers, France, pp. 19–23 (2021)

22. Warg, F., Blom, H., Borg, J., Johansson, R.: Continuous deployment for dependable systems with continuous assurance cases. In: 2019 IEEE International Symposium on Software Reliability Engineering Workshops (ISSREW), pp. 318–325 (2019). https://doi.org/10.1109/ISSREW.2019.00091

23. Wozniak, E., Cârlan, C., Acar-Celik, E., Putzer, H.J.: A safety case pattern for systems with machine learning components. In: Casimiro, A., Ortmeier, F., Schoitsch, E., Bitsch, F., Ferreira, P. (eds.) SAFECOMP 2020. LNCS, vol. 12235, pp. 370–382. Springer, Cham (2020). https://doi.org/10.1007/978-3-030-55583-2_28

STARS: A Tool for Measuring Scenario Coverage When Testing Autonomous Robotic Systems

Till Schallau[1]([✉]) [iD], Dominik Mäckel[1] [iD], Stefan Naujokat[1] [iD],
and Falk Howar[1,2] [iD]

[1] TU Dortmund University, Dortmund, Germany
till.schallau@tu-dortmund.de
[2] Fraunhofer ISST, Dortmund, Germany

Abstract. Extensive testing and simulation in different environments has been suggested as one piece of evidence for the safety of autonomous systems, e.g., in the automotive domain. To enable statements on the absolute number or fractions of tested scenarios, methods and tools for computing their coverage are needed. In this paper, we present STARS, a tool for specifying semantic environment features and measuring scenario coverage when testing autonomous systems.

1 Introduction

Autonomous systems are envisioned to operate in open and complex environments. Assuring the safety of systems in such environments is still an open challenge [14]. We rely on structured arguments (i.e., safety cases) about the safety of autonomous systems and test deployments for assessing the safety before rolling systems out at a large scale. One function of test deployments is to collect data for the estimation of reasonable risk by exposing the system to many different environments. The UL 4600 norm, e.g., lists the coverage of an operational design domain (ODD) as a mandatory aspect of testing automated systems [2]. There, an ODD specifies environment conditions (e.g., infrastructure, weather), under which an autonomous system is designed to operate [1]. Even before releasing prototypes into test deployments, we need to be reasonably sure of their safety.

To this end, scenario-based testing methods have been developed over the past couple of years [10,20,21]. While there is a strong focus on the automotive domain, case studies range from validating the safety of robotic systems [9], to generating accident scenarios [11], to testing of a nautic collision avoidance system [15], to testing the safe behavior of unmanned aerial vehicles in urban environments [19].

At both stages, it is important to decide whether the system was exposed to sufficiently many environments (or scenarios). There is, however, currently a lack of methods for measuring the degree of exposure to different environments or the coverage of scenarios. A prerequisite of measuring coverage is the definition of features that constitute different scenarios.

B. Sangchoolie et al. (Eds.): EDCC 2024 Workshops, CCIS 2078, pp. 62–70, 2024.
https://doi.org/10.1007/978-3-031-56776-6_6

We have developed a conceptual framework, called STARS, for specifying scenario classifiers, determining the number of potentially observable scenarios, and measuring their coverage by analyzing data recorded by the system under test [18]. The STARS framework has so far been applied to different data sources in the field of automated driving systems. In previous works [18], we analyzed data generated with the CARLA [4] and other simulators. In ongoing projects, we analyze the KITTI dataset [7] containing real world driving data, and conduct a case study on a platooning controller for model-size vehicles.

In this paper, we present the STARS tool that we have developed to aid the analysis of environment coverage in different case studies. STARS automates the coverage analysis for user-defined application domains. It allows users to specify semantic environment features in a metric-time first order logic over observations and to construct scenario classifiers from these features. Moreover, the tool provides statistics over feature combinations, and can identify the absence of feature expressions in recorded data, enabling test coverage-driven test scenario selection. STARS is publicly available as open-source software.[1]

Related Work. Hildebrandt et al. present an approach for counting the number of unique environments experienced by an automated driving system [8]. In contrast to our work, they compute classifying signatures directly on sensor data and do not specify or compute semantic features. As a consequence, they analyze saturation but not coverage. Amersbach and Winner [3] present a method for defining the required test coverage of autonomous driving systems. They propose functional descriptions of scenarios that are similar to our predicate definitions. They do not provide an implementation. Li et al. [12] introduce the open-source research tool ComOpT which is capable of generating concrete scenarios based on higher-class descriptions of scenarios. While generating these scenarios, the framework maximizes the coverage of k-way combinatorial testing. Majumdar et al. [13] take a similar approach with their PARACOSM tool and domain-specific language for defining and instantiating scenario components. Esterle et al. [6] formalize traffic rules for highway situations by using Linear Temporal Logic (LTL). They use Spot [5] to transform the defined formulas into deterministic finite automata. Rizaldi et al. [16] also use LTL formulas for monitoring traffic rules. They provide their formalizations as rules in Isabelle/HOL. All these works do not aim at coverage.

Outline. The remainder of the paper is structured as follows. Section 2 starts with an overview over the STARS tool. Section 2.1 describes how the it can be customized for particular domains, before showing the specification of features in Sect. 2.2 and the construction of classifiers in Sect. 2.3. Section 3 demonstrates the data analysis process and the computed metrics.

2   The STARS Tool

Figure 1 shows the data artifacts, specification formalisms, and processors involved when using the STARS tool. Only the two boxes depicted on the left

---

[1] https://github.com/tudo-aqua/stars.

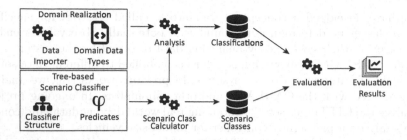

Fig. 1. Overview of the STARS coverage analysis tool (Icons licensed under CC BY 4.0 https://fontawesome.com/license/free)

need to be provided by users of the framework. While STARS already provides reusable realizations for some domains, the tool is generally designed to be domain-agnostic.

The first step when using STARS is to set it up for the targeted application domain (cf. Sect. 2.1), requiring two artifacts: the first artifact describes the *domain data types*, a data structure that abstractly captures properties of relevant entities (e.g., cars, robots, etc.) and the world they operate in (e.g., ground type, weather, etc.). Technically, this is done by implementing corresponding interfaces provided by the framework. STARS is implemented in Kotlin. Thus, any compatible JVM-based language (such as Java) can be used. The second artifact is a *data importer* that reads recorded data (e.g., from simulations or system deployments) and instantiates the domain data types. While the tool does not restrict the type of data that is imported this way, in our case-studies, we relied on the automatic binding of JSON format files to data classes.

The second step in the framework usage is modeling features of the operational design domain (ODD) of the analyzed autonomous system. Features can, e.g., be specified over data streams in formal logic (cf. Sect. 2.2). STARS provides a specification and decision implementation for the linear Counting Metric First-Order Temporal Binding Logic (CMFTBL) [18], but the tool allows for arbitrary computations of feature expression. Individual features can then be combined into tree-based classifiers that model combinatorial combinations of features as a basis for classifying perceived environments into scenario classes (cf. Sect. 2.3). Based on the tree-based classifiers, valid combinations of features can be calculated by STARS. These combinations form all possible scenario classes. Segments of recorded data can then be classified into one of these classes. During data analysis, the observed classifications and the set of possible scenario classes are computed. The tool provides implementations of various metrics and analyses, e.g., scenario class coverage, feature occurrence, scenario instance count, and missing features expressions (cf. Sect. 3), but also allows for the implementation of custom metrics for an application domain.

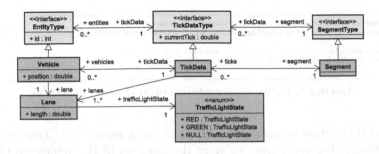

Fig. 2. Simple realization of the data types for an automated driving system

2.1   Instantiating STARS for an Operational Design Domain

To apply the framework to analyze recorded data of an autonomous system, it has to be instantiated first. In order to analyze data from various domains with STARS, the following parts have to be adapted.

Domain Data Types. The imported domain data has to implement the interfaces of the tool's generic data structure. On the top level, STARS requires a set of *segments*, which are the analysis units to be classified. The segments each hold a list of *ticks* in chronological order, where each tick holds a set of *entity* states for the tick's particular timestamp. Since the analysis is based on discrete events, the ticks' time distance (i.e., the sensor sampling rate) has to be selected such that no feature may occur in between. Additional domain information may also be added to the implementations of these basic data types. The domain data types are used to define the predicates used for classifying the data.

Predicates. To automatically analyze the recorded data, environment features need to be modeled and evaluated in a programmable manner. Therefore, existing temporal logics (cf. Sect. 2.2) or other specification and evaluation methods can be used to phrase and evaluate predicates for different scenario features. They are used to express domain properties that can be evaluated based on the given domain data.

TSC. In order to define the ODD of the autonomous system, the defined predicates are structured hierarchically using Tree-based Scenario Classifiers (TSC) (cf. Sect. 2.3). As every analyzed autonomous system has different intended functionalities and differing environments in which they have to operate, a dedicated TSC has to be defined. Additionally, the underlying logic evaluation system (cf. Sect. 2.2) and the evaluation metrics (cf. Sect. 3) can be replaced, making the STARS framework highly customizable for the applied domain.

To demonstrate the adaptability of STARS to different domains, we give a simple example of an implementation for the domain data types in Fig. 2. The three interfaces printed in green (i.e., *EntityType*, *TickDataType*, and *SegmentType*) show the generic data structure of the tool, while the domain-specific classes are printed in blue. For simplicity reasons, the implementing classes *Vehicle*, *TickData*, and *Segment* only contain minimal information about a vehicle's

```
1   val hasRelevantRedLight = predicate(Vehicle::class){ ctx, v ->
2     eventually(v) { v -> hasRedLight.holds(ctx, v) && isAtEndOfRoad.holds(ctx, v) }
3   }
4   val hasRedLight = predicate(Vehicle::class){ ctx, v ->
5     v.lane.trafficLightState == TrafficLightState.RED
6   }
```

Listing 1. Kotlin implementation of predicates (1) and (2)

state and its relation to classes modeling the environment (i.e., *Lane* and *TrafficLightState*). For every tick, we store the position of the vehicle on the lane it is driving on relative to the lane's length as well as the traffic light state for each lane. The available states are defined by the set {*RED, GREEN, NULL*}. State *NULL* indicates that there is no traffic light for the lane. They are later used to demonstrate the definition of predicates (cf. Sect. 2.2). A simple scenario classifier based on this domain data structure is given in Sect. 2.3.

2.2 Specifying Environment Features

For feature classification, STARS supports implementations of various logics, or evaluations, as long as they are executable on or callable from the JVM and utilize the implemented domain data types (cf. Sect. 2.1). The tool already implements the CMFTBL logic, which we introduced in a previous work [18]. An example property expressed in CMFTBL over our minimal domain data model (cf. Fig. 2) is to check for a *relevant red light*. A relevant red light is observed if at any point in time the traffic light belonging to the lane the vehicle v is driving on shows red. We also require v to be at the end of the road, which we define to hold if v has a distance of 3 m or less to the end of its current lane. If *hasRelevantRedLight* evaluates to *true*, the feature is present in the analyzed segment. The predicate is formally defined in (1), hierarchically using predicates (2) and (3).

$$hasRelevantRedLight(v) := \Diamond(hasRedLight(v) \wedge isAtEndOfRoad(v)) \qquad (1)$$

$$hasRedLight(v) := v.lane.trafficLightState = RED \qquad (2)$$

$$isAtEndOfRoad(v) := v.pos \geq v.lane.length - 3 \qquad (3)$$

These predicates can be directly implemented using the CMFTBL implementation provided by STARS, which supplies all required logical operators (i.e., *eventually, globally,* etc.) as Kotlin extension functions. Listing 1 illustrates the Kotlin implementation of predicates (1) and (2) to demonstrate how to express hierarchic predicate definitions. Predicate (3) follows analogously.

2.3 Constructing Scenario Classifiers from Features

We briefly introduce Tree-based Scenario Classifiers (TSCs) and how the tool supports their definition. A TSC describes a tree structure in which each node represents one feature that should be classified. An edge that is connected to a

```
1  TSC(root<Vehicle, TickData, Segment>{
2    all("Root"){
3      exclusive("Traffic Density"){
4        leaf("High Traffic"){condition = {ctx->hasHighTrafficDensity.holds(ctx)}}
5        leaf("Middle Traffic"){condition = {ctx->hasMidTrafficDensity.holds(ctx)}}
6        leaf("Low Traffic"){condition = {ctx->hasLowTrafficDensity.holds(ctx)}}
7      }
8      bounded("Traffic Light", (0 to 1)){
9        leaf("Has Green Light"){condition = {ctx->hasRelevantGreenLight.holds(ctx)}}
10       leaf("Has Red Light"){condition = {ctx->hasRelevantRedLight.holds(ctx)}}
11     }
12     exclusive("Maneuver"){
13       leaf("Lane Change"){condition = {ctx->changedLane.holds(ctx)}}
14       leaf("Lane Follow"){condition = {ctx->followsLane.holds(ctx)}}
15     }
16   }
17 })
```

Listing 2. Kotlin implementation of the TSC from Figure 3

node requires a predicate which should evaluate to the boolean value *true* iff the feature represented by the node is present. Evaluating all predicates of a TSC for a given data segment results in a concrete TSC instance classifying the scenario that was observed in the analyzed segment. Consistency checking of the TSC is ongoing research and has to be ensured by the user for now.

The nodes of the TSC are furthermore annotated with multiplicity constraints, which provide an upper and lower bound for the number of child nodes in a TSC instance, to ensure the validity of the data and correctness of the predicates. An example TSC is given in Fig. 3. Different multiplicity constraints (A: All, X: Exclusive) and ranges (0..1) are used to ensure data integrity and the correct combination of predicates. These bounds are used to calculate all valid predicate combinations (i.e., scenario classes), and

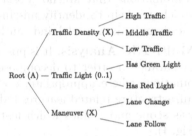

Fig. 3. Example Tree-Based Classifier

therefore TSC instances, that are observable. For example, an X constraint only allows exactly one related predicate to be valid. Therefore, predicates at edges originating from a node marked with X may never occur simultaneously. This means that the total amount of possible instances only increases by the number of predicates under the node, in contrast to an optional node (marked with O; not in this example) that allows for all combinations of those predicates. For the mathematical calculations of the combination count, we refer the interested reader to [18]. Listing 2 shows the implementation of the TSC.

3 Measuring Scenario Coverage

STARS uses evaluation components for computing scenario coverage and other metrics (cf. Fig. 1) on classified segments of recorded data and supports the export of computed results to structured text files and plots. For some framework metrics, such as the saturation over time of the *scenario class coverage* for TSCs (cf. Fig. 4)[2], pre-defined plots are provided.

Coverage and other Metrics. The unique contribution of STARS is the capability to compute *scenario class coverage*, the percentage of scenario classes that is present in a data set. The metric is computed by calculating the number of possible scenario classes and by counting observed ones. Other evaluation components count feature expressions, and compute the distribution of features and feature combinations. The *scenario class count* and the related *scenario class distribution* are useful for analyzing saturation over time and long-tail distribution of scenarios. STARS identifies scenario classes and feature combinations that are not observed,

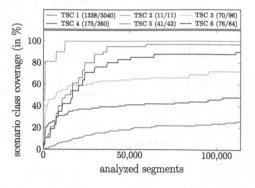

Fig. 4. The *scenario class coverage* metric plot, showing the coverage progress for six TSCs. The legend also details the amount of occurred unique scenario classes and possible scenario classes.

which can help to identify missing test cases. These metrics are independent of the domain data model and can be used in every analysis with STARS.

Multi-TSC Analysis. It is possible to define multiple TSCs and analyze them in parallel in order to decompose the combinatorial explosion of feature combinations where appropriate, e.g., to analyze coverage of weather-related and infrastructure-related features independently. Each TSC then specifies the analysis scope and defines which features are relevant for the current analysis (cf. Fig. 4).

Customization. Finally, users can define new plots, as STARS uses the lets-plot library that supports a variety of diagrams and plots. With custom evaluation components, domain-specific metrics over the domains' specific data models (e.g., average flight altitude in aeronautics) can equally be analyzed.

References

1. Taxonomy and definitions for terms related to driving automation systems for on-road motor vehicles. Standard J3016, SAE International (2021). https://www.sae.org/standards/content/j3016_202104/
2. Standard for safety for the evaluation of autonomous products. Standard ANSI/UL 4600-2023, UL Standards & Engagement (2023). https://ul.org/UL4600
3. Amersbach, C., Winner, H.: Defining required and feasible test coverage for scenario-based validation of highly automated vehicles. In: ITSC 2019, IEEE (2019). https://doi.org/10.1109/itsc.2019.8917534

---

[2] Note: The data model used for the evaluation of the TSCs is described in [17].

4. Dosovitskiy, A., Ros, G., Codevilla, F., Lopez, A., Koltun, V.: CARLA: an open urban driving simulator. In: PMLR 2017, vol. 78. PMLR (2017). https://proceedings.mlr.press/v78/dosovitskiy17a.html
5. Duret-Lutz, A., Lewkowicz, A., Fauchille, A., Michaud, T., Renault, É., Xu, L.: Spot 2.0 — a framework for LTL and ω-automata manipulation. In: Artho, C., Legay, A., Peled, D. (eds.) ATVA 2016. LNCS, vol. 9938, pp. 122–129. Springer, Cham (2016). https://doi.org/10.1007/978-3-319-46520-3_8
6. Esterle, K., Gressenbuch, L., Knoll, A.C.: Formalizing traffic rules for machine interpretability. In: CAVS 2020, IEEE (2020). https://doi.org/10.1109/CAVS51000.2020.9334599
7. Geiger, A., Lenz, P., Stiller, C., Urtasun, R.: Vision meets robotics: The KITTI dataset. Int. J. Robot. Res. (IJRR) **32**(11), 1231–1237 (2013). https://doi.org/10.1177/0278364913491297
8. Hildebrandt, C., von Stein, M., Elbaum, S.: PhysCov: physical test coverage for autonomous vehicles. In: ISSTA 2023, ACM (2023). https://doi.org/10.1145/3597926.3598069
9. Huck, T.P., Ledermann, C., Kröger, T.: Simulation-based testing for early safety-validation of robot systems. In: SPCE 2020, IEEE (2020). https://doi.org/10.1109/SPCE50045.2020.9296157
10. ISO central secretary: road vehicles - safety of the intended functionality. Standard ISO 21448:2022, International Organization for Standardization (2022). https://www.iso.org/standard/77490.html
11. Jenkins, I.R., Gee, L.O., Knauss, A., Yin, H., Schroeder, J.: Accident scenario generation with recurrent neural networks. In: ITSC 2018, IEEE (2018). https://doi.org/10.1109/itsc.2018.8569661
12. Li, C., Cheng, C.H., Sun, T., Chen, Y., Yan, R.: ComOpT: combination and optimization for testing autonomous driving systems. In: ICRA 2022, IEEE (2022). https://doi.org/10.1109/icra46639.2022.9811794
13. Majumdar, R., Mathur, A., Pirron, M., Stegner, L., Zufferey, D.: Paracosm: a language and tool for testing autonomous driving systems. Technical Report arXiv:1902.01084, arXiv (2021). https://doi.org/10.48550/arXiv.1902.01084
14. Mariani, R.: An overview of autonomous vehicles safety. In: IRPS 2018, IEEE (2018). https://doi.org/10.1109/irps.2018.8353618
15. Porres, I., Azimi, S., Lilius, J.: Scenario-based testing of a ship collision avoidance system. In: SEAA 2020, IEEE (2020). https://doi.org/10.1109/SEAA51224.2020.00090
16. Rizaldi, A., et al.: Formalising and monitoring traffic rules for autonomous vehicles in Isabelle/HOL. In: Polikarpova, N., Schneider, S. (eds.) IFM 2017. LNCS, vol. 10510, pp. 50–66. Springer, Cham (2017). https://doi.org/10.1007/978-3-319-66845-1_4
17. Schallau, T., Naujokat, S.: Validating behavioral requirements, conditions, and rules of autonomous systems with scenario-based testing. Electron Communications of the EASST **82** (2023). https://doi.org/10.14279/tuj.eceasst.82.1222
18. Schallau, T., Naujokat, S., Kullmann, F., Howar, F.: Tree-based scenario classification: a formal framework for coverage analysis on test drives of autonomous vehicles. Technical Report arXiv:2307.05106, arXiv (2023). https://doi.org/10.48550/arXiv.2307.05106, submitted to NFM 2024
19. Schmidt, T., Hauer, F., Pretschner, A.: Understanding safety for unmanned aerial vehicles in urban environments. In: IV 2021, IEEE (2021). https://doi.org/10.1109/IV48863.2021.9575755

20. Weber, H., et al.: A framework for definition of logical scenarios for safety assurance of automated driving. Traffic Injury Prev. **20**(sup1) (2019). https://doi.org/10.1080/15389588.2019.1630827
21. Weng, B., Capito, L., Ozguner, U., Redmill, K.: Towards guaranteed safety assurance of automated driving systems with scenario sampling: an invariant set perspective. IEEE Trans. Intell. Veh. **7**(3) (2022). https://doi.org/10.1109/tiv.2021.3117049

Workshop on Blockchain Technology and Artificial Intelligence in Smart Cities (TRUST IN BLOCKCHAIN)

Workshop on Blockchain Technology and Artificial Intelligence in Smart Cities (TRUST IN BLOCKCHAIN)

Workshop Description

The TRUST IN BLOCKCHAIN workshop aimed to investigate the role of trust in the implementation of digital technologies by means of an interdisciplinary approach, including engineering, economic, and legal considerations. The main focus is the use of Artificial Intelligence and Blockchain Technology (BCT) in Smart cities and in particular in smart energy systems, as means to optimize energy trading and management. They are key technologies for energy transition that require technological challenges to be faced for their implementation (e.g. cyber security), but they also raise further critical issues about how to secure the trust process in terms of requirements of the legal framework, technical applications, and economic/business conditions. The main topics of the workshop are cyber security, BCT in peer-to-peer energy trading, and artificial intelligence methods for energy supply coordination.

This workshop has been conceived in the context of the TRUST RISE project ("TRUST" digital TuRn in EUrope: Strengthening relational reliance through Technology – H2020 MSCA RISE 2021–2025). The project deals with understanding the role of trust in the implementation of digital technologies and suggesting actual means of development. Special attention is devoted to Blockchain Technology (BCT) as one of the most relevant forms of Distributed Ledger Technology (DLT). With a multi-disciplinary approach, the mutual relationship between trust and DLT in order to evaluate how to implement trust in people-to-people, people-to-business, and people-to-authorities relations is addressed.

We aim to take a multi-disciplinary point of view about this topic, by including also contributions looking into social, economic, and legal aspects in addition to technical issues. Dependable Computing and AI and blockchain represent a convergence of technologies and efforts aimed at enhancing the dependability, security, and efficiency of critical systems and applications within Europe, leveraging the capabilities of AI and blockchain technologies. This convergence aligns with broader European initiatives to promote innovation, sustainability, and regulatory compliance in emerging technology domains.

Organization

Program Chairs

Alessia Arteconi   KU Leuven, Belgium
Adriano Mancini   Università Politecnica delle Marche, Italy

Program Committee

Marco Baldi   Università Politecnica delle Marche, Italy
Marcella Cornia   Unimore, Italy
Geert Deconinck   KU Leuven, Belgium
Emanuele Frontoni   Università di Macerata, Italy
Joaquin Garcia-Alfaro   Télécom SudParis Institut
                                    Mines-Télécom & Institut
                                    Polytechnique de Paris, France
Wissam Mallouli   Montimage, France
Francesca Spigarelli   Università di Macerata, Italy

Spatial-Temporal Graph Neural Network for Detecting and Localizing Anomalies in PMU Networks

Tohid Behdadnia(✉) ⬤, Klaas Thoelen⬤, Fairouz Zobiri⬤, and Geert Deconinck⬤

Department of Electrical Engineering (ESAT-ELECTA), KU Leuven, Leuven, Belgium
{tohid.behdadnia,klaas.thoelen,fairouz.zobiri,
geert.deconinck}@kuleuven.be

Abstract. The role of phasor measurement unit (PMU) data as real-time indicators of system dynamics is critically important for accurate state estimation in power systems. PMUs, being cyber-physical devices, are susceptible to cyberattacks, such as false data injection (FDI). As FDI can lead to incorrect state estimation and subsequent destructive impacts, the prompt detection of falsified data is crucial to preclude such adverse outcomes. In response to this challenge, this paper introduces a spatial-temporal graph neural network (ST-GNN) for the detection and localization of anomalies in the PMU network. The model incorporates a convolutional neural network and long short-term memory units, which are adept at extracting spatial and temporal features effectively. The inclusion of graph-based analysis in our model significantly improves the understanding of interconnections between neighboring PMUs, thereby enhancing its precision in detecting and pinpointing anomalies, even under sophisticated stealth false data injection attacks. The performance of this framework has been thoroughly evaluated on two IEEE test systems, the 39-bus and 127-bus systems, across a variety of attack scenarios. The results from these evaluations affirm the high accuracy of the model, highlighting its potential as a reliable tool for safeguarding power systems against cyber-physical threats.

Keywords: Anomaly Detection · Cyber-Security · False Data Injection · Graph Neural Network (GNN) · Long Short-Term Memory (LSTM)

1 Introduction

1.1 Cyber-Attacks on Power Systems

Power systems critically depend on the accuracy and reliability of their state estimation units (SEUs), which utilize real-time measurements to assess the grid's operational status. [1]. These estimations are pivotal for the efficient management and control of power systems. However, the integration of information and communication technology (ICT) systems and cyber-physical devices (e.g. phasor measurement units (PMUs)) in power networks, renders SEUs vulnerable to cyber threats. Compromised data can significantly impact the precision of state estimations, posing a substantial threat to power grid integrity [2].

B. Sangchoolie et al. (Eds.): EDCC 2024 Workshops, CCIS 2078, pp. 75–82, 2024.
https://doi.org/10.1007/978-3-031-56776-6_7

The increasing sophistication of cyberattacks, motivated by economic incentives, the potential for severe service disruptions, and risks to critical infrastructure, has resulted in the advancement of attack methodologies and an increase in their success rates [3, 4]. This heightened sophistication has even rendered commonly used bad data detection (BDD) methods inadequate in countering advanced techniques such as stealth false data injection (SFDI) [5, 6].

Given these challenges, the vulnerability of SEUs to sophisticated cyber threats, especially stealthy data manipulation tactics, becomes a critical issue in maintaining the security and reliability of power grids.

1.2 Advanced Methods for Identifying SFDI

A multitude of research endeavors have delved into understanding the methodologies of attackers, subsequently proposing appropriate defensive strategies to effectively counter these advanced attack techniques. For example, Ashok et al. [7] explored the vulnerability of power grid state estimators to SFDI attacks, proposing an online anomaly detection algorithm using load forecasts, generation schedules, and synchrophasor data. Pang et al. [8] focused on detecting SFDI attacks in networked control systems through active data modification, a novel approach challenging traditional methods. Similarly, Boyaci et al. [9] introduced a detection methodology using graph neural networks (GNN) for smart grids, enhancing the precision of identifying stealthy attacks. Ashrafuzzaman et al. [10] presented an ensemble-based machine learning approach, tested on the IEEE 14-bus system, demonstrating the effectiveness of integrating multiple classifiers. Lastly, Chen et al. [11] proposed a sophisticated two-step detection method using a deep autoencoding Gaussian mixture model, emphasizing the balance between risk production and detection prevention in practical attack policies.

These studies collectively reveal that data-driven and machine learning (ML) methods are highly effective in countering SFDI attacks, due to their adaptability in the rapidly evolving cyber threat environment.

1.3 Motivation and Contributions

Confronting the sophisticated challenges posed by SFDI attacks, and informed by the demonstrated success of data-driven and ML algorithms in mitigating these threats, this paper introduces a spatial-temporal graph neural network (ST-GNN) as a robust approach for identifying anomalies in PMU data. By integrating graph-based analytics, our model significantly improves the understanding of interconnections among PMUs, thereby enhancing the accuracy of detecting complex and stealthy attacks.

To validate the effectiveness and adaptability of our proposed model, extensive evaluations were conducted on various power systems with different sizes and different numbers of PMUs. These evaluations confirmed the accuracy and flexibility of our approach, underlining its potential in advancing SFDI detection methodologies.

2 Theoretical Foundations

2.1 Attack Model

The relationship between the sensor reading vector Z and the system state vector X can be described as [12]:

$$Z = h(X) + E \tag{1}$$

where:

- Z is a vector denoted as $Z = [z_1, z_2, \ldots, z_m]^T$, representing the sensor readings, where z_i is the i-th sensor reading.
- X is a vector representing the system state, given as $X = [V_1, V_2, \ldots, V_y; \theta_1, \theta_2, \ldots, \theta_y]^T$, where V_i and θ_i are the magnitudes and phase angles of bus voltages for the i-th bus in the power system.
- $h(\cdot)$ is a vector of nonlinear functions that map the system state X to the sensor readings Z.
- E is a vector denoted as $E = [e_1, e_2, \ldots, e_m]^T$, representing the vector of measurement errors.

The estimated system state $\hat{X}$ is computed using the weighted least squares as:

$$\hat{X} = argmin_X [Z - h(X)]^T R^{-1} [Z - h(X)] \tag{2}$$

here, R represents the measurement error covariance matrix.

To assess the potential error or corruption in a measurement, a ℓ_2-norm detector is utilized. It involves verifying whether the following condition holds:

$$\|r\| = \|Z - h(\hat{X})\| \geq \tau \tag{3}$$

where, τ represents a predefined threshold for the norm of the measurement residual vector r.

In accordance with [13], a potential threat arises when an adversary possesses advanced knowledge of the network architecture and the ability to simultaneously access and manipulate a set of measurements. This scenario could potentially lead to the circumvention of BDD algorithms. However, it is imperative to elucidate that such an occurrence is contingent upon specific conditions, which are explained in the following discussion. Following an FDI attack, the SEU can generate an inaccurate system state estimate $\hat{X}_a = \hat{X} + C$ by introducing a tampered measurement $Z_A = Z + A$. Here, A denotes the attack vector, and C represents intentional errors deliberately added to the system's estimations $\hat{X}$. If the vector Z can bypass BDD, then Z_A can also evade BDD, provided that $A = h(\hat{X} + C) - h(\hat{X})$. This stems from the mathematical verification affirming the constancy of the measurement residual's likeness between Z_A and the original measurement:

$$\|r_A\| = \|Z_A - h(\hat{X}_A)\| = \|Z + A - h(\hat{X} + C)\|$$
$$= \|Z + A - h(\hat{X} + C) + h(\hat{X}) - h(\hat{X})\| = \|r + A - h(\hat{X} + C) + h(\hat{X})\| = \|r\| \leq \tau \tag{4}$$

As a consequence, it can be deduced that sole reliance on BDD proves inadequate in safeguarding against SFDI attacks. Throughout the scope of this paper and the ensuing investigation, we employ SFDI attack strategies derived from the principles delineated in (4).

2.2 ST-GNN for Anomaly Detection (Proposed Method)

This section delves into the comprehensive architectural design of the proposed ST-GNN model. This model uniquely amalgamates GNN, long short-term memory (LSTM), and convolutional neural network (CNN) layers [14]. This integration is engineered to apprehend and analyze both spatial and temporal dynamics within a network resembling the distribution of PMUs. The overarching structure of the proposed methodology is illustrated in Fig. 1. Subsequently, an in-depth exposition of the individual functionalities of each constituent layer employed in this architecture is provided.

GNN Layer: The first layer of the proposed ST-GNN architecture is the GNN layer, designed to process graph-structured data by updating the representation of each node based on its neighboring nodes. Mathematically, for a graph $G = (\mathcal{N}, \mathcal{O})$ with nodes $n \in \mathcal{N}$ and edges $(u, n) \in \mathcal{O}$, each node n has an initial feature vector. The GNN layer updates the feature vector of each node n by aggregating features of its neighboring nodes as follows:

$$x_n^{(l+1)} = \sigma\left(\hat{D}^{-\frac{1}{2}}\hat{A}\hat{D}^{-\frac{1}{2}}x_n^{(l)}W^{(l)}\right) \tag{5}$$

where $x_n^{(l)}$ is the matrix of node features at layer l, $\hat{A}$ is the adjacency matrix of the graph with an added self-loop, $\hat{D}$ is the degree matrix of $\hat{A}$, $W^{(l)}$ is the trainable weight matrix of layer l, and σ is a non-linear activation function.

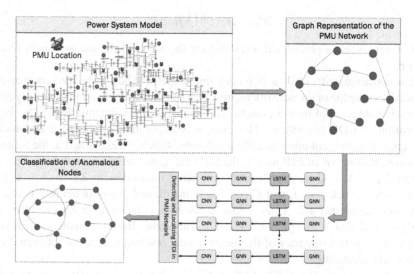

Fig. 1. ST-GNN for detecting and localizing SFDI attacks in a PMU network.

LSTM Layer: To effectively capture the temporal dependencies intrinsic to sequential PMU data, our architecture integrates a LSTM layer. This layer operates on a sequence of feature vectors $\{f_1, f_2, \ldots, f_t\}$, each vector representing node features at a distinct time point. The LSTM, comprising input, output, and forget gates, alongside a candidate memory cell (refer to Fig. 2.), methodically updates its hidden state HS_t and cell state CS_t at each time step t. The update process is governed by the following set of equations:

$$\text{Forget gate: } \mathcal{F}_t = sigmoid\left(W_{\mathcal{F}} \cdot [HS_{t-1}, f_t] + b_{\mathcal{F}}\right) \tag{6}$$

$$\text{Input gate: } i_t = sigmoid\left(W_i \cdot [HS_{t-1}, f_t] + b_i\right) \tag{7}$$

$$\text{Output gate: } o_t = sigmoid\left(W_o \cdot [HS_{t-1}, f_t] + b_o\right) \tag{8}$$

$$\text{Cell state update: } \widetilde{CS}_t = \tanh\left(W_{CS} \cdot [HS_{t-1}, f_t] + b_{CS}\right) \tag{9}$$

$$\text{New cell state: } CS_t = \mathcal{F}_t \odot CS_{t-1} + i_t \odot \widetilde{CS}_t, \{\odot \rightarrow \text{Hadamard Product}\} \tag{10}$$

$$\text{New hidden state: } HS_t = o_t \odot \tanh(CS_t) \tag{11}$$

where W and b represent the trainable weight and bias parameters, respectively, of the LSTM layer.

CNN Layer: The final component in our architecture is a CNN layer. This layer is adept at processing grid-like structured data and is employed to extract higher-level spatial features from the graph representation. For a feature map $\mathcal{Z}$ obtained from the previous layers, the CNN layer applies convolutional filters W_{cnn} to extract spatial features as follows:

$$\mathcal{Z}_{out} = \sigma\left(W_{cnn} * \mathcal{Z} + b_{cnn}\right) \tag{12}$$

where $*$ represents the convolution operation, and b_{cnn} is the bias term associated with each filter.

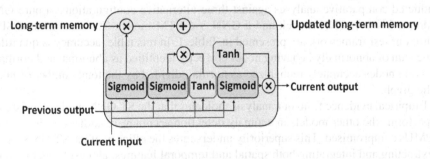

Fig. 2. LSTM unit architecture.

It is worth mentioning that in the ST-GNN framework, we have devised, specifically architected for real-time or near-real-time analysis, the dual processes of anomaly detection and localization are seamlessly integrated into a unified workflow. This means that when nodes are classified as 'normal' or 'abnormal' in the final stage of our model, it also concurrently reveals the locations of specific nodes that are affected by SFDI attacks. This integrated approach significantly enhances the system's efficiency by enabling simultaneous detection and precise localization of anomalies within the network, a crucial feature in scenarios where rapid response to security threats is imperative.

3 Case Study on the Test System

3.1 Generation of Attack-Free and Falsified Measurements

In this research, two distinct electrical power system test models are employed: the 39-bus New England test system, featuring 10 generators, and the 127-bus Western Systems Coordinating Council (WSCC) test system, comprising 39 generators. This study presumes the strategic placement of PMUs to ensure complete system observability, thereby facilitating the acquisition of system state variables, specifically, the magnitudes and angles of bus voltages, via state estimation. Adhering to the optimal PMU placement methodology delineated in Reference [15], the placement results in equipping 14 buses in the 39-bus system and 39 buses in the 127-bus system with PMUs. The PMUs operate at a data reporting rate of 60 samples per second, equivalent to one sample per cycle in a 60 Hz electrical system.

The simulation framework developed for this study models the dynamics of these power systems under variable load conditions, with incremental adjustments of 5%, spanning from 80% to 120% of nominal load. This simulation generated a total of 32,000 scenarios, wherein 5% to 100% of the PMUs were subjected to cyber-attacks. These attacks were designed to avoid detection by the bad data detection (BDD) mechanisms, as elaborated in Sect. 2.1 of the paper.

Ultimately, the dataset was partitioned into three subsets for training, validation, and testing, in a ratio of 4:2:1, respectively.

3.2 Results

To elucidate the significance of each component within our proposed ST-GNN model, we conducted comparative analyses against three alternative configurations: a pure GNN model, a GNN + CNN model, and a GNN + LSTM model. The outcomes of SFDI within our test framework are presented in Table 1. In this table, accuracy is quantified as the sum of abnormally behaving nodes correctly identified as abnormal and normally behaving nodes accurately recognized as normal, divided by the total number of nodes in the graph.

Empirical evidence from our analysis indicates that the ST-GNN model consistently outperforms the other models in anomaly detection accuracy, regardless of the number of PMUs compromised. This superiority underscores the efficacy of the ST-GNN model in extracting and integrating both spatial and temporal features, alongside adept feature aggregation, to enhance the learning of dependencies in measurement data for more precise anomaly detection.

Table 1. Accuracy rates (%) for anomaly detection in PMU networks under various ratios of PMUs affected by SFDI attacks.

Proportion of PMUs Subject to SFDI Attack	39-bus Test System				127-bus Test System			
	GNN	GNN + CNN	GNN + LSTM	ST-GNN	GNN	GNN + CNN	GNN + LSTM	ST-GNN
~5%	97.31	97.36	98.56	**99.89**	96.22	96.38	96.98	**99.56**
~10%	97.30	97.34	98.55	**99.70**	96.16	96.24	96.89	**99.10**
~25%	97.07	97.29	98.50	**99.65**	96.05	96.18	96.83	**99.01**
~50%	96.90	97.09	98.23	**99.33**	95.77	96.01	96.62	**98.71**
~75%	96.00	96.46	97.50	**99.20**	94.01	95.11	96.02	**98.34**
~90%	94.14	94.54	96.99	**98.88**	91.77	91.99	94.95	**97.56**
100%	80.99	83.23	90.90	**97.23**	75.81	76.30	91.43	**96.09**

4 Conclusion

This study presents a comprehensive examination of anomaly detection in PMUs within cyber-physical power systems, leveraging an ST-GNN framework. Specifically, the research integrates GNN, LSTM networks, and CNN to effectively identify sophisticated SFDI attacks, which are capable of evading conventional BDD methods. The efficacy of each constituent layer in enhancing detection accuracy is elucidated through comparative analysis against three distinct architectural configurations. The findings demonstrate that the ST-GNN model consistently achieves significant performance in anomaly detection, irrespective of the number of compromised PMUs or the scale of the power system. Future work will involve extending the current model to include additional input features, such as network traffic data, for the early detection of anomalies. This enhancement is aimed at precluding attacks from reaching the physical layer (power system layer) by identifying them at their earlier stage in the communication network layer (ICT layer).

Acknowledgments. The work presented in this paper was conducted within the framework of two projects: the TRUST project (https://trust-rise.eu/), which received funding from the European Union's Horizon 2020 research and innovation program under the Marie Skłodowska-Curie grant agreement No 101007820*, and the CYPRESS project (https://cypress-project.be), supported by the FPS Economy of Belgium through the Energy Transition Funds.

{*Disclaimer: This article reflects only the author's view and the REA is not responsible for any use that may be made of the information it contains}.

Disclosure of Interests. The authors have no competing interests to declare that are relevant to the content of this article.

References

1. Zhao, J., et al.: Power system dynamic state estimation: motivations, definitions, methodologies, and future work. IEEE Trans. Power Syst. **34**, 3188–3198 (2019)
2. Musleh, A.S., Chen, G., Dong, Z.Y., Wang, C., Chen, S.: Vulnerabilities, threats, and impacts of false data injection attacks in smart grids: an overview. In: 2020 International Conference on Smart Grids and Energy Systems (SGES) (2020)
3. Reda, H.T., Anwar, A., Mahmood, A.: Comprehensive survey and taxonomies of false data injection attacks in smart grids: attack models, targets, and impacts. Renew. Sustain. Energy Rev. **163**, 112423 (2022)
4. Behdadnia, T., Thoelen, K., Zobiri, F., Deconinck, G.: Leveraging deep learning to increase the success rate of DOS attacks in PMU-based automatic generation control systems. IEEE Trans. Ind. Inform., 1–14 (2024). https://doi.org/10.1109/TII.2023.3342413
5. Zhang, J., Chu, Z., Sankar, L., Kosut, O.: False data injection attacks on phasor measurements that bypass low-rank decomposition. In: 2017 IEEE International Conference on Smart Grid Communications (SmartGridComm) (2017)
6. Chu, Z., Zhang, J., Kosut, O., Sankar, L.: Unobservable false data injection attacks against pmus: Feasible conditions and multiplicative attacks. In: 2018 IEEE International Conference on Communications, Control, and Computing Technologies for Smart Grids (SmartGridComm) (2018)
7. Ashok, A., Govindarasu, M., Ajjarapu, V.: Online detection of stealthy false data injection attacks in power system state estimation. IEEE Trans. Smart Grid, **9**, 1636–1646 (2016)
8. Pang, Z.-H., Fan, L.-Z., Sun, J., Liu, K., Liu, G.-P.: Detection of stealthy false data injection attacks against networked control systems via active data modification. Inf. Sci. **546**, 192–205 (2021)
9. Boyaci, O., Narimani, M.R., Davis, K.R., Ismail, M., Overbye, T.J., Serpedin, E.: Joint detection and localization of stealth false data injection attacks in smart grids using graph neural networks. IEEE Trans. Smart Grid **13**, 807–819 (2022)
10. Ashrafuzzaman, M., Das, S., Chakhchoukh, Y., Shiva, S., Sheldon, F.T.: Detecting stealthy false data injection attacks in the smart grid using ensemble-based machine learning. Comput. Secur. **97**, 101994 (2020)
11. Chen, C., et al.: Data-driven detection of stealthy false data injection attack against power system state estimation. IEEE Trans. Industr. Inf. **18**, 8467–8476 (2022)
12. Abur, A., Expósito, A.G.: Power System State Estimation: Theory and Implementation. Marcel Dekker, New York (2004)
13. Liu, Y., Ning, P., Reiter, M.K.: False data injection attacks against state estimation in electric power grids. ACM Trans. Inf. Syst. Secur. **14**, 1–33 (2011)
14. Wu, Y., Dai, H.-N., Tang, H.: Graph neural networks for anomaly detection in industrial internet of things. IEEE Internet Things J. **9**, 9214–9231 (2022)
15. Gou, B.: Generalized integer linear programming formulation for optimal PMU Placement. IEEE Trans. Power Syst. **23**, 1099–1104 (2008)

On the Application of Blockchain Technology in Microgrids

Maarten Evens[1,2](✉) ⓘ, Patricia Ercoli[3] ⓘ, and Alessia Arteconi[1,2,3] ⓘ

[1] KU Leuven, 3000 Leuven, Belgium
maarten.evens@kuleuven.be
[2] EnergyVille, 3600 Genk, Belgium
[3] Università Politecnica delle Marche, 60131 Ancona, Italy

Abstract. To further integrate renewable energy resources into the electricity grids, increasing the consumption of locally produced electricity is one of the key solutions to reduce the operational cost of the future energy system. Therefore, the local and intelligent principles of microgrids in which users can directly exchange energy with other local users via peer-to-peer energy trading functionalities for flexible energy management are of paramount importance. Regarding peer-to-peer energy trading, setting up a virtual trading network for users can be realised via several communication and database mechanisms, in which the focus of the current work is on the application of the blockchain technology. This article aims to shed a light on the required actions and implementation efforts such as pricing mechanisms, privacy constraints, scalability and on the required overarching energy management system. By overviewing the available literature on the application of blockchain technology, this article also aims to provide a critical view on the applicability of this particular technology for peer-to-peer energy trading purposes.

Keywords: Blockchain · Microgrid · Peer-to-Peer Energy Trading · P2P

1 Introduction

The negative aspects of global warming initiated the energy transition with ambitious goals of several governments to reach carbon neutrality by 2050 [1, 2]. To this aim, a few large fossil-fired power plants are being replaced by distributed renewable energy production technologies such as solar panels and wind turbines, while the consumption side is being electrified by transitioning to zero-emission technologies such as heat pumps and electric vehicles. However, the weather-dependency, volatility and simultaneity of several renewable technologies puts additional stress on the electricity grids and requires the paradigm shift to a scenario where the energy demand follows the energy production. In light of this, implementing the principles of microgrids and transactive energy systems [3, 4] are promising solutions as a large power grid is divided into smaller neighbourhoods in which participants communicate in an automated and coordinated manner to exchange energy with the creation of value and maintaining the grid in reliable working conditions as main overarching goals [5–8].

B. Sangchoolie et al. (Eds.): EDCC 2024 Workshops, CCIS 2078, pp. 83–90, 2024.
https://doi.org/10.1007/978-3-031-56776-6_8

For the implementation of transactive energy microgrid communication, distributed ledger technologies (DLTs) are seen as a potential solution to allow a privacy-friendly, secure, reliable and trustworthy information exchange technology between several grid users and related parties. These technologies record and store transactions into a digital ledger, which is distributed among all participants. Its decentralised character without requiring a middlemen or centralised party is widely recognised in literature to offer a transparent, secure and immutable tool for peer-to-peer networks [9]. Regarding the available platforms, M. F. Zia et al. [3] distinguished six main platforms (Blockchain, Directed Acyclic Graph, Hashgraph, Holochain, Tempo and Corda) and concluded that the blockchain technology is mainly adopted for various applications. The current article focusses on the application of blockchain technology and aims to provide a critical overview on its applicability and required mechanisms to enable flexible energy management in future microgrids. To this end, multiple blockchain projects and trading platforms are studied.

2   Communication and Interaction via Blockchain Technology

Figure 1 introduces a conceptual overview of physical connections in a transactive energy microgrid, including the communication interactions with the blockchain technology.

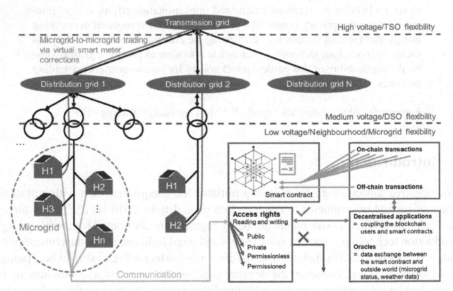

Fig. 1. Transactive microgrid communication. An overview of the physical grid connections and communication requirements to interact with the blockchain technology [10].

On a whole system analysis, Zia et al. [3] distinguished a seven layer system architecture, encompassing layers related to the user, network, system operator, market, distributed ledger, communication and regulation. Regarding the interaction with the ledger, a first selection process on the reading access (public or private) and writing access (permissionless or permissioned) ensures that only allowed users (e.g. users from a certain microgrid) can enter and make transactions on the ledger. Depending on the approach, public, private or hybrid ledgers exists [11, 12] for which the hybrid approach is expected to fit well for peer-to-peer energy trading purposes as it combines the advantages of public and private ledgers.

After having determined the access rights, several aspects have to be further clarified before moving to an operational stage. Indeed, multiple studies reviewed and further clarified aspects such as smart contracts [13], architectures/frameworks [3, 14], and challenges/opportunities [15–17]. However, the mechanisms required to interact with the blockchain itself are mainly neglected, while Fig. 1 shows that an additional number of three communication levels after having passed the reading/writing access have to be implemented [10].

A first level includes Decentralised Applications or DApps [18], which mainly come as web-based applications to enable grid users to easily interact with the blockchain platform.

Given its distributed nature, aimed at securing peer-to-peer transactions, blockchains are in fact not directly able to retrieve external inputs (e.g. weather data, price data, energy predictions) or send outputs directly to its users (e.g. agreed price and energy volumes). Hence, a second required intermediate level includes the so-called Oracles [19] and enable to exchange information between the blockchain network and the outside world. However, this also initiates the Oracle Problem as blockchains are fundamentally based on not requiring any middleman, while introducing Oracles leads to including a third party in the network [20] and a careful selection is required.

Finally, the third communication level deals with how transactions are effectively written into the blockchain, for which on-chain and off-chain transactions can be distinguished. Given that transaction fees are commonly adopted to reward network validators for their transaction validation work and availability, reducing the number of transactions is common. On-chain transactions can be seen as submitting each individual transaction to the network. In contrast, off-chain transactions are not directly initiated on the blockchain itself, but require to set up an external channel between several users. Once all required transactions are performed, the channel is closed and only the final balances of each user are written into the chain, thus limiting the transaction cost.

3   Flexible Energy Trade in Microgrids

Blockchain technology plays a key role in decentralising local microgrid markets, empowering consumers to actively choose their energy sources [8]. This decentralisation is enabled by a peer-to-peer (P2P) database network, which creates a transparent and secure platform for two-way energy transactions. Prosumers, coordinated through the blockchain, engage in near real-time energy exchanges based on production conditions and grid reliability [3, 8].

Several peer organisation models, including fully decentralised, community-based, and composite approaches, define market structures for P2P trading [21]. In fully decentralised markets, participants engage in direct over-the-counter exchanges through bilateral contracts [21, 22], providing flexibility in configuring trading systems according to economic, social, and environmental preferences [23–25]. Community-based trading involves a community manager who facilitates the exchange of energy in which stakeholders can participate collaboratively [26] or competitively [27], whereas composite markets allow stakeholders to interact across different organisational structures while maintaining their own properties [21].

Regardless of the peer organisation model, the blockchain platform facilitates the decentralisation of P2P microgrids by enabling data management and storage without the need for a central authority [28, 29] and automates the real-time evaluation of flexible energy resources. These independent entities, such as storage systems, efficient technologies, and demand response strategies, aim to maximise their interests through automated transaction matching [30]. Blockchain's support for smart contracts further improves coordination between system operators, distributed energy resources and energy consumers. Blockchain technology automates interactions within electricity markets, providing a communication system for entities involved in the sale, transmission, and management of electricity [3, 8, 31]. By combining blockchain with sensors and smart appliances, energy assets and flexibility services are verified and stored securely. The technology also facilitates real-time balancing in microgrids and enables efficient transactive energy services [32].

Electricity pricing is a key element in the efficient and flexible operation of microgrids, and the introduction of blockchain significantly shapes this by influencing demand by keeping track of fluctuations in price signals. Various pricing mechanisms, from direct over-the-counter trading [21, 22] to auction-based approaches [33, 34], enhance transparency and data validation. Optimisation tools, including game theory and constrained optimisation, contribute to effective market clearing and distributed energy resources (DERs) allocation [21, 33, 35–38].

The integration of blockchain technology into the energy sector is reshaping the landscape by introducing decentralised solutions for P2P energy trading, microgrid management, and demand response. In this sense, several active projects exemplify the practical application of blockchain in P2P energy trading and microgrid management:

- FlexiDAO [39]: Focusses on the aggregation and control of flexible DERs, enhancing grid operation efficiency through transparent and secure energy flexibility. The platform incentivises collaboration among participants.
- Spectral [40]: Offers solutions for energy trading, market platform integration, and automation of bidding processes. It integrates various energy assets, including solar, wind, batteries, and cogeneration, optimising trading strategies.
- Electron [41]: Provides a flexible market infrastructure for interaction among grid operators and DERs. The platform enables mutual negotiation and response to intraday variations, supporting multiple market services.
- EVShare Foundation [42]: A technology partnership promoting sustainable ridesharing powered by clean energy. The platform securely engages multiple participants through distributed applications and a public application programming interface (API).
- LO3 Energy [43]: Facilitates innovative P2P distributed energy solutions, with the Brooklyn Microgrid project utilising DLT and tokens for transactive energy services.

- Leap [44]: An aggregator platform for DER flexibility providers, offering virtual microgrids to balance the grid. The platform ensures real-time energy trading, smart meter synchronisation, and advanced bidding strategies.

4 Conclusion

This article aimed to provide a critical review on available works focussed on the adoption of blockchain technology in the energy sector and more specifically for peer-to-peer energy trading purposes. It is concluded that many works in literature deal with the overall microgrid system architecture, potential applications such as lowering the total energy cost, increasing the self-consumption of a neighbourhood, pricing strategies and advantages related to the adoption of the blockchain technology. Literature shows a clear advantage of peer-to-peer energy trading in microgrids in which blockchain technology can play an important role to guarantee privacy, security and transparency. However, future work is still required before reaching a large-scale adoption as the exact implementation of setting up the communication with the blockchain technology is a first missing aspect for which more attention is needed. Points requiring a more in-depth description are on-chain and off-chain transactions and, communication of the blockchain transactions to the outside world to activate energy management systems in order to meet the commitment. Furthermore, more attention should be given on which information is exactly stored on the chain. Majority of the studies describe the adoption of the blockchain technology, but remain vague on if the full energy trading process is obtained directly on the chain or if trading agreements are realised via classical supply-demand balancing mechanisms and only the final agreement is stored on the chain. However, these aspects are of tremendous importance when transitioning from simulation studies to field trials. Finally, future work is also required on the required energy balancing mechanisms when users do not meet their commitments once energy is traded as most works assume perfect predictions.

Acknowledgements. This project has received funding from the European Union's Horizon 2020 research and innovation program under the Marie Skłodowska-Curie grant agreement No. 101007820. This publication reflects only the author's view, and the REA is not responsible for any use that may be made of the information it contains.

Disclosure of Interests. The authors have no competing interests to declare that are relevant to the content of this article.

References

1. Strategy EU: Communication RW Policy priorities for the fit for 55 package. 32:23643001178–02
2. European Commission: European Green Deal. In: 52019DC0640 (2019). https://eur-lex.eur opa.eu/legal-content/EN/TXT/?qid=1588580774040&uri=CELEX:52019DC0640
3. Zia, M.F., Benbouzid, M., Elbouchikhi, E., Muyeen, S.M., Techato, K., Guerrero, J.M.: Microgrid transactive energy: review, architectures, distributed ledger technologies, and market analysis. IEEE Access **8**, 19410–19432 (2020). https://doi.org/10.1109/ACCESS.2020.296 8402

4. Huang, Q., et al.: A review of transactive energy systems: concept and implementation. Energy Rep. **7**, 7804–7824 (2021). https://doi.org/10.1016/j.egyr.2021.05.037
5. Thukral, M.K.: Emergence of blockchain-technology application in peer-to-peer electrical-energy trading: a review. Clean Energy **5**, 104–123 (2021). https://doi.org/10.1093/ce/zkaa033
6. Woodhall, A.: How Blockchain can Democratize Global Energy Supply. Elsevier Inc. Amsterdam (2018)
7. Wang, J., Wang, Q., Zhou, N., Chi, Y.: A novel electricity transaction mode of microgrids based on blockchain and continuous double auction. Energies (Basel) **10**, 1–22 (2017). https://doi.org/10.3390/en10121971
8. Mengelkamp, E., Gärttner, J., Rock, K., Kessler, S., Orsini, L., Weinhardt, C.: Designing microgrid energy markets: a case study: The Brooklyn Microgrid. Appl. Energy **210**, 870–880 (2018). https://doi.org/10.1016/J.APENERGY.2017.06.054
9. Ahl, A., Yarime, M., Tanaka, K., Sagawa, D.: Review of blockchain-based distributed energy: implications for institutional development. Renew. Sustain. Energy Rev. **107**, 200–211 (2019). https://doi.org/10.1016/j.rser.2019.03.002
10. Evens, M., Ercoli, P., Arteconi, A.: Blockchain-Enabled Microgrids: Toward Peer-to-Peer Energy Trading and Flexible Demand Management (2023). https://doi.org/10.3390/en16186741
11. Hu, J., Reed, M.J., Al-Naday, M., Thomos, N.: Hybrid Blockchain for IoT-Energy Analysis and Reward Plan (2021). https://doi.org/10.3390/s21010305
12. Baqer Mollah, M., et al.: Blockchain for future smart grid: a comprehensive survey. IEEE Internet Things J. **8** (2021). https://doi.org/10.1109/JIOT.2020.2993601
13. Kirli, D., et al.: Smart contracts in energy systems: a systematic review of fundamental approaches and implementations. Renew. Sustain. Energy Rev. **158**, 112013 (2022). https://doi.org/10.1016/j.rser.2021.112013
14. Hasankhani, A., Mehdi Hakimi, S., Shafie-khah, M., Asadolahi, H.: Blockchain technology in the future smart grids: a comprehensive review and frameworks. Int. J. Electr. Power Energy Syst. **129**, 106811 (2021). https://doi.org/10.1016/J.IJEPES.2021.106811
15. Andoni, M., et al.: Blockchain technology in the energy sector: a systematic review of challenges and opportunities. Renew. Sustain. Energy Rev. **100**, 143–174 (2019). https://doi.org/10.1016/j.rser.2018.10.014
16. Hrga, A., Capuder, T., Zarko, I.P.: Demystifying distributed ledger technologies: limits, challenges, and potentials in the energy sector. IEEE Access **8**, 126149–126163 (2020). https://doi.org/10.1109/ACCESS.2020.3007935
17. Tushar, W., et al.: Peer-to-peer energy systems for connected communities: a review of recent advances and emerging challenges. Appl. Energy **282** (2021). https://doi.org/10.1016/j.apenergy.2020.116131
18. Suthar, S., Pindoriya, N.M.: Blockchain and smart contract based decentralized energy trading platform. In: 2020 21st National Power Systems Conference, NPSC 2020 (2020). https://doi.org/10.1109/NPSC49263.2020.9331883
19. Condon, F., Martinez, J.M., Kim, Y.C., Ahmed, M.A.: EnergyAuction: oracle blockchain-based energy trading system for microgrids. In: IEEE Conference on Power Electronics and Renewable Energy, CPERE 2023, pp. 1–6 (2023). https://doi.org/10.1109/CPERE56564.2023.10119578
20. Caldarelli, G.: Overview of blockchain oracle research. Future Internet **14** (2022). https://doi.org/10.3390/fi14060175
21. Tushar, W., Saha, T.K., Yuen, C., Smith, D., Poor, H.V.: Peer-to-peer trading in electricity networks: an overview. IEEE Trans Smart Grid **11**, 3185–3200 (2020). https://doi.org/10.1109/TSG.2020.2969657

22. Next: What is OTC trading? (2023). https://www.next-kraftwerke.com/knowledge/what-is-otc-trading. https://www.next-kraftwerke.com/knowledge/what-is-otc-trading. Accessed 27 Aug 2023
23. Gajic, D.B., Petrovic, V.B., Horvat, N., Dragan, D., Stanisavljevic, A., Katic, V.: Blockchain-based smart decentralized energy trading for grids with renewable energy systems. In: 2021 21st International Symposium on Power Electronics (Ee), pp. 1–7. IEEE (2021)
24. Raja, A.A., Grammatico, S.: Bilateral peer-to-peer energy trading via coalitional games. IEEE Trans. Industr. Inform. **19**, 6814–6824 (2023). https://doi.org/10.1109/TII.2022.3196339
25. Sorin, E., Bobo, L., Pinson, P.: Consensus-based Approach to Peer-to-Peer Electricity Markets with Product Differentiation
26. Moret, F., Pinson, P.: Energy collectives: a community and fairness based approach to future electricity markets. IEEE Trans. Power Syst. **34**, 3994–4004 (2019). https://doi.org/10.1109/TPWRS.2018.2808961
27. Tushar, W., et al.: Energy storage sharing in smart grid: a modified auction-based approach. IEEE Trans Smart Grid **7**, 1462–1475 (2016). https://doi.org/10.1109/TSG.2015.2512267
28. Wu, Y., Wu, Y., Cimen, H., Vasquez, J.C., Guerrero, J.M.: P2P energy trading: blockchain-enabled P2P energy society with multi-scale flexibility services. Energy Rep. **8**, 3614–3628 (2022). https://doi.org/10.1016/j.egyr.2022.02.074
29. Soto, E.A., Bosman, L.B., Wollega, E., Leon-Salas, W.D.: Peer-to-peer energy trading: a review of the literature. Appl. Energy **283**, 116268 (2021). https://doi.org/10.1016/j.apenergy.2020.116268
30. Xu, Z., Wang, Y., Dong, R., Li, W.: Research on multi-microgrid power transaction process based on blockchain Technology. Electr. Power Syst. Res. **213**, 108649 (2022). https://doi.org/10.1016/j.epsr.2022.108649
31. Junaidi, N., Abdullah, M.P., Alharbi, B., Shaaban, M.: Blockchain-based management of demand response in electric energy grids: a systematic review. Energy Rep. **9**, 5075–5100 (2023). https://doi.org/10.1016/J.EGYR.2023.04.020
32. Lucas, A., Geneiatakis, D., Soupionis, Y., Nai-Fovino, I., Kotsakis, E.: Blockchain technology applied to energy demand response service tracking and data sharing. Energies (Basel) **14**, 1881 (2021). https://doi.org/10.3390/en14071881
33. Das, A., Peu, S.D., Akanda, M., Islam, A.: Peer-to-peer energy trading pricing mechanisms: towards a comprehensive analysis of energy and network service pricing (NSP) mechanisms to get sustainable enviro-economical energy sector. Energies (Basel) **16**, 2198 (2023). https://doi.org/10.3390/en16052198
34. Liu, N., Yu, X., Wang, C., Li, C., Ma, L., Lei, J.: Energy-sharing model with price-based demand response for microgrids of peer-to-peer prosumers. IEEE Trans. Power Syst. **32**, 3569–3583 (2017). https://doi.org/10.1109/TPWRS.2017.2649558
35. Foti, M., Vavalis, M.: Blockchain based uniform price double auctions for energy markets. Appl. Energy **254**, 113604 (2019). https://doi.org/10.1016/j.apenergy.2019.113604
36. Moniruzzaman, M., Yassine, A., Benlamri, R.: Blockchain and cooperative game theory for peer-to-peer energy trading in smart grids. Int. J. Electr. Power Energy Syst. **151**, 109111 (2023). https://doi.org/10.1016/J.IJEPES.2023.109111
37. An, J., Lee, M., Yeom, S., Hong, T.: Determining the Peer-to-Peer electricity trading price and strategy for energy prosumers and consumers within a microgrid. Appl. Energy **261**, 114335 (2020). https://doi.org/10.1016/J.APENERGY.2019.114335
38. Doan, H.T., Cho, J., Kim, D.: Peer-to-peer energy trading in smart grid through blockchain: a double auction-based game theoretic approach. IEEE Access **9**, 49206–49218 (2021). https://doi.org/10.1109/ACCESS.2021.3068730
39. FlexiDAO (2017) FlexiDAO. https://www.flexidao.com/. Accessed 28 Aug 2023
40. Spectral: Stellar (2015). https://spectral.energy/. Accessed 28 Aug 2023

41. Electron: Electron (2015). https://electron.net/. Accessed 28 Aug 2023
42. EVShare Foundation: EVShare (2018). https://evshare.com/. Accessed 28 Aug 2023
43. LO3 Energy: LO3 Energy (2012). https://lo3energy.com/. Accessed 28 Aug 2023
44. Leap: Leap (2018). https://www.leap.energy/. Accessed 28 Aug 2023

Power System Transient Stability Prediction in the Face of Cyber Attacks: Employing LSTM-AE to Combat Falsified PMU Data

Benyamin Jafari[✉] and Mehmet Akif Yazici

Information and Communications Research Group, Informatics Institute,
Istanbul Technical University, Istanbul, Turkey
{jafari16,yazicima}@itu.edu.tr

Abstract. Phasor measurement units (PMUs) are essential instruments in delivering real-time data crucial for monitoring the dynamics of power systems. They are widely used in transient stability prediction (TSP), significantly contributing to the effective maintenance of power systems post-contingency stability. The accuracy and reliability of data derived from PMUs are crucial for the effective execution of TSP. However, the PMU data is at risk of being compromised by false data injection (FDI) attacks. Such vulnerabilities could lead to a significant degradation in the reliability of the data, potentially resulting in the misdirection of algorithms tailored for TSP. In response to this challenge, this article presents a resilient approach for TSP capable of functioning effectively under FDI attacks. Utilizing a long short-term memory autoencoder (LSTM-AE), our proposed method is engineered to proficiently capture and learn the normative spatial and temporal correlations and patterns present in time-series PMU data, across both steady-state and transient operational states. Consequently, this approach facilitates the algorithmic reconstruction and rectification of PMU measurements that have been compromised due to FDI, thereby upholding the robustness of the TSP process in the face of cyber threats. The performance of the proposed method is validated using the IEEE 39-bus system, subjected to a wide array of scenarios. This rigorous testing demonstrates the algorithm's robustness and effectiveness in maintaining accurate TSP in scenarios where the integrity of PMU data is professionally compromised to avoid easy detection or reconstruction.

Keywords: Cyber-Physical Security · False Data Injection (FDI) · Long Short-Term Memory (LSTM) · Autoencoders (AE) · Phasor Measurement Units (PMUs) · Transient Stability Assessment

1 Introduction

Due to the stressed operating conditions, compounded by increasing load demands and further exacerbated by the unprecedented integration of renewable energy sources and electric vehicle fast-charging stations, modern power systems are now more vulnerable to credible contingencies. Such contingencies, under certain conditions, can initiate a domino effect of protective measures, potentially escalating into extensive cascading failures, and in extreme cases, leading to widespread blackouts [1, 2].

© The Author(s), under exclusive license to Springer Nature Switzerland AG 2024
B. Sangchoolie et al. (Eds.): EDCC 2024 Workshops, CCIS 2078, pp. 91–103, 2024.
https://doi.org/10.1007/978-3-031-56776-6_9

To mitigate the aforementioned risks, recent developments have pivoted towards leveraging data-driven approaches, especially machine learning (ML) and deep learning (DL), for the rapid transient stability prediction (TSP) of power systems, enabling rapid and efficient control responses. These ML/DL-based TSP models are predominantly utilized for their ability to extract informative features from raw phasor measurement unit (PMU) data (synchrophasor measurements) and to learn the complex relationship between the stability status of a power system and its time-series measurable quantities in extremely short time intervals following a disturbance [3–6]. However, the PMU network, being integral in providing input for TSP models, embodies a fusion of cyber and physical components. This dual nature renders them attractive targets for cyber-physical attacks [7–10]. Such attacks aim to compromise the performance of TSP algorithms, thus posing a significant threat to the stability and reliability of power systems.

The body of literature examining the vulnerability of PMUs to FDI attacks provides critical insights into the complexities and security challenges prevalent in modern power systems. In a noteworthy research contribution [11], the study unveiled the capability of imperceptible FDI attacks to circumvent conventional bad data detectors (BDD), primarily reliant on measurement residuals for their operation. This revelation was substantiated by demonstrating the ineffectiveness of detection mechanisms founded on low-rank decomposition, thereby emphasizing a substantial vulnerability within prevailing detection systems and catalyzing the demand for advanced and more resilient detection methodologies. Further extending this discourse, another study [12] critically evaluated the effectiveness of traditional BDDs in detecting FDI attacks targeted at PMUs. This research proposed an enhanced BDD model that incorporates the dynamics of zero injection buses, thereby augmenting the detector's capacity to identify conditions under which FDI attacks may remain undetectable. This finding suggests that the integration of additional analytic parameters can substantially bolster the resilience of PMUs against such cyber-attacks. In parallel, Alexopoulos et al. [13] conducted an analytical exploration focusing on the role of zero injection buses as potential vectors for the execution of FDI attacks on PMUs within power network infrastructures. In a related study [14], Chu et al. investigated the direct physical impacts of FDIs on N-1 reliable power technology, underscoring the necessity for real-time contingency analysis and the implementation of secure power dispatch strategies. These studies collectively underscore the potential for exploitation of both the physical infrastructure and operational protocols within power networks, revealing a layered and complex vulnerability landscape. Moreover in reference [15], the susceptibility of both DC and AC estimators to FDI attacks was meticulously scrutinized, with a specific focus on PMU-based state estimation. This investigation demonstrated that PMUs, when compared within this context, are vulnerable to FDI threats, thus illuminating the widespread risk across various types of estimators.

The observed expansion in the scope of vulnerability, transitioning from specific PMU models to a broader susceptibility across various power system state estimators, highlights the critical need for the formulation and implementation of robust and effective techniques dedicated to the accurate detection and subsequent correction of data compromised by FDI attacks.

Several studies have explored various methods for detecting FDI attacks on PMUs. One approach utilized traditional ML algorithms for detecting false data traces in PMU data streams [16]. While these methods can be effective in certain scenarios, they often lack the capability to capture complex sequential and temporal patterns, which are key in identifying sophisticated FDI attacks. The method proposed in [12] improves the detection of unobservable FDI attacks but may still be limited in dealing with highly sophisticated attacks that are designed to mimic normal system behaviors. Further, a new approach for detecting and correcting false data in PMU measurements was proposed in [17], which operates independently of SCADA measurements. However, this method's effectiveness in dynamically changing data environments and transient states can be challenging.

Building upon existing scholarly work in the realm of FDI detection, this study acknowledges the inherent complexities and obstacles involved in rectifying data affected by FDI attacks. In response to these challenges, the paper introduces a robust methodology that utilizes a long short-term memory autoencoder (LSTM-AE) model. This model is specifically crafted to rectify data that has been distorted by FDI attacks. Once the data is amended using the LSTM-AE, it is then integrated into TSP models. The primary objective of this preprocessing step with the LSTM-AE, followed by feeding the corrected data into TSP models, is to empirically demonstrate how such corrective measures can significantly enhance the performance and effectiveness of TSP algorithms, especially when they operate in environments compromised by FDI attacks. Thus, this approach not only addresses the immediate issue of data reliability post-attack but also contributes to the broader discourse on improving the resilience of TSP models in the face of FDI attacks.

This paper's principal contributions are as follows:

- This research delineates the marked decline in the reliability of PMU data when subjected to falsification, emphasizing its subsequent impact on the efficacy of TSP models. The findings highlight the correlation between compromised PMU data and the diminished accuracy of TSP outcomes, offering valuable insights into the importance of enhancing data integrity in power systems.
- The paper presents a robust methodology employing an LSTM-AE specifically developed for preprocessing and correcting PMU data prior to their application in TSP models. The efficacy of this approach is substantiated by the enhanced performance and precision of TSP models, particularly in scenarios where they are exposed to FDI attacks aimed at bypassing traditional BDDs.

The rest of this paper is organized as follows: In Sect. 2, we delve into the discussion of the power system under FDI attacks and measurement issues. Section 3 explores the understanding of autoencoders and the necessity for using LSTM units for learning normative spatial and temporal correlations and patterns present in PMU data. Section 4 presents the details of the proposed model and simulation results, and, in conclusion, Sect. 5 summarizes this article.

2 Power System Under FDI Attack and Measurement Issues

In this section, we examine preliminary theoretical constructs related to the impacts of FDI attacks on time series PMU measurements and key power system quantities that are integral to the system's stability.

2.1 Impact of FDI Attack on PMU Measurements

In power systems, voltage and current signals are mathematically expressed as:

$$U(k) = |u|cos(2\pi fk\tau + \angle u) \tag{1}$$

$$I(k) = |I|cos(2\pi fk\tau + \angle I) \tag{2}$$

where $|u|$, $|I|$, $\angle u$, $\angle I$, f, τ, and k are voltage magnitude, current magnitude, voltage angle, current angle, signal frequency, fixed sampling time, and sampling index respectively. These formulas represent the signals' dynamics in the time domain. For real-time monitoring, PMUs initially acquire voltage and current signals from voltage and current transformers (CTs and VTs) across all phases of the power grid. These PMUs employ a phase-locked loop to synchronize with the system's frequency, crucial for accurate frequency tracking. After synchronization, PMUs use Clarke and Park transformations to convert the three-phase signals into a two-phase format in the $d - q$ axis. In this $d - q$ frame, PMUs measure the magnitude, frequency, and phase angle of electrical quantities. Subsequently, these measurements traverse a wide-area network (WAN) and are transmitted to a central control center in the form of packets conforming to the IEEE C37.118.2 standard. This standard currently lacks specified security mechanisms to defend against cyber-attacks. While efforts have been made to integrate security-enhancing measures into IEEE C37.118.2, there remain numerous vulnerabilities in the data transmission process over WANs, leaving openings for potential manipulation of transmitted packets by attackers. This study, however, does not delve into the specific techniques utilized for such manipulations. For the purposes of this discussion, it is presumed that attackers possess sufficient access to alter these packets, though the detailed methods employed to acquire this access are not extensively examined.

The repercussions of packet manipulations manifest in altered voltage magnitude ($|u|$) and current magnitude ($|I|$), as well as variations in voltage angle ($\angle u$) and current angle ($\angle I$) and frequency (f), as demonstrated in the following equations:

$$|u|_{att} = |u|_{alt} + |u| \tag{3}$$

$$|I|_{att} = |I|_{alt} + |I| \tag{4}$$

$$\angle u_{att} = \angle u_{alt} + \angle u \tag{5}$$

$$\angle I_{att} = \angle I_{alt} + \angle I \tag{6}$$

$$f_{att} = f_{alt} + \angle f \tag{7}$$

where the subscripts "*att*" and "*alt*" denote the values of the respective quantities after an attack and the amount of shift or alteration in that quantity, respectively.

2.2 Impact of FDI Attack on Power System Stability

Transient stability deals with the system's ability to maintain synchronism following a large disturbance, such as a fault or sudden change in load. The key equation for transient stability is often expressed through the swing equation:

$$H.\frac{d\delta}{dt} = P_m - P_e \tag{8}$$

where H, δ, t, P_m, and P_e is the system inertia constant, rotor angle, time, mechanical power input, and electrical power output, respectively. During a disturbance, such as a fault, the P_m and P_e may become temporarily imbalanced. If the P_m exceeds the P_e significantly and is not adequately controlled, the rotor angle (δ) will undergo acceleration, signaling an indication of instability. Hence, it is imperative to accurately calculate the P_e in real-time and adjust the P_m accordingly.

The determination of P_e in real time involves utilizing PMU measurements, as outlined:

$$P_e = |u||I|\cos(\angle u - \angle I) \tag{9}$$

In the presence of a false data injection attack, the P_e can be represented as:

$$P_{eatt} = |u|_{att}|I|_{att}\cos(\angle u_{att} - \angle I_{att}) \tag{10}$$

This implies that $P_{eatt} \neq P_e$, and indicates that an incongruity exists between the actual (P_e) and corrupted value (P_{eatt}) of electrical power. Such a disparity can lead to inaccuracies in P_m adjustment, subsequently the rotor angle (δ) may experience acceleration, contributing to instability.

ML/DL-based TSP models are employed to learn the complex relationship between real-time PMU measurements and rotor angle dynamics, with the objective of accurately forecasting rotor angle acceleration behavior to avert instability; however, the risk of misinformation due to falsified measurements can pose a significant challenge, potentially misleading these ML/DL-based TSP models and leading to ineffective control actions.

3 Understanding Autoencoders and the Need for LSTM Units

3.1 Autoencoders

Autoencoders (AE) are a type of deep neural network designed to reconstruct a given input through encoding and decoding processes. The encoder compresses the input into a latent space representation, and the decoder reconstructs the original input from this encoded representation. AEs are trained to find a robust representation of the input, enabling the recovery of the original data from the noise.

The encoding (ψ) and decoding (ϕ) processes can be modeled with nonlinear feature mapping functions, f_e (for encoding) and f_d (for decoding), using trainable weight and bias matrices (Θ_e and Θ_d). Stacked AEs, which include multiple hidden layers, aim to minimize the reconstruction residual, enhancing the ability to learn high-level data features. However, AEs lack the capacity to handle temporal dependencies in the data. Thus, recurrent neural networks (RNNs) are used in conjunction with AEs to capture temporal relationships in sequence data.

3.2 LSTM Neural Network

LSTM neural networks are capable of retrieving information from previous time steps and updating data in internal memory cells at each step. This characteristic enables LSTMs to recognize time-dependent relationships in data sequences. An LSTM unit's output at each time step is determined by its memory cell state, intermediate output, and the input at that step.

As shown in Fig. 1 the LSTM architecture includes input, output, and forget gates, as well as a candidate memory cell. These components collectively decide what information to retain or discard, allowing the network to map temporal correlations in data over time. When LSTM units are incorporated within an AE network, they enable the capturing of spatiotemporal correlations in data sequences. This results in a learning model capable of reconstructing input sequences with minimal reconstruction residuals, and hence, effectively detecting deviations from normal system dynamics.

4 Case Study on the Test System

To evaluate the efficacy of the proposed mitigation methodology for injected false data employing LSTM-AE, the New England IEEE 39 bus system is utilized. This power system configuration encompasses 34 transmission lines, 12 transformers, and 19 dynamic loads, in addition to ten synchronous machines equipped with speed governors and excitation systems, all operating at a frequency of 60 Hz. The aggregate complex power of the system approximates 6500 megavolt-amperes (MVA). Moreover, 10 PMUs are positioned within the generation units. Comprehensive system parameters are delineated in [18].

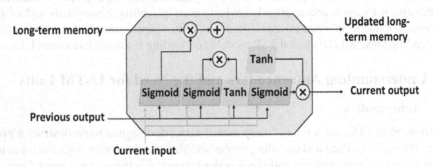

Fig. 1. LSTM unit architecture.

The simulation of the New England system in this study is accomplished through a time-domain hybrid simulation methodology, as proposed in [3]. The adoption of hybrid simulation is justified as it represents a more realistic approach to generating synthetic synchrophasor data. This choice stems from the inherent challenges associated with obtaining real-life PMU data from industrial sources, where concerns pertaining to data security and confidentiality may pose impediments.

4.1 Data Generation

To ensure the reliability of the model, it is imperative that the dataset encompasses a comprehensive array of dynamics. Our simulation endeavors to emulate the power system's behavior under diverse load levels, incorporating incremental adjustments of five percent, spanning the range from 80 to 120%. Additionally, the analysis accounts for symmetrical faults on all buses and lines as credible contingencies. The initiation time of the fault (t_f) and the operational duration of the circuit breaker are established at 0.02 s and 4–10 cycles, respectively. Consequently, the fault-clearing time (t_c) is defined as $t_c = [(0.02 + \frac{4}{60})s, (0.02 + \frac{10}{60})s]$. Subsequent to a time-domain simulation of 40 s, each simulated scenario is assigned a class label 0 (stable) or 1 (unstable) according to:

$$L = \begin{cases} 1 & for \quad \eta \leq 0 \\ 0 & for \quad \eta > 0 \end{cases} \tag{11}$$

The stability index η is derived from power angle measurements, specifically by analyzing the maximum angular separation between any pair of generators simultaneously during the post-fault response [3, 19]. This index serves as a criterion for assessing whether any generator within the system has deviated from synchronous operation.

The simulation generates 32,000 samples with a stable-to-unstable ratio of approximately 2:1. To rectify the class imbalance and mitigate the risk of overfitting, random under-sampling is employed, resulting in an adjusted stable-to-unstable ratio of 1:1. Subsequently, the remaining 18,000 samples are randomly partitioned into training and test sets in a 2:1 ratio.

Inspired by the techniques described in reference [11], FDI is applied to both the training and test sets. The resulting falsified training dataset is then utilized as input for the LSTM-AE, which undergoes training to reconstruct the original, unfalsified data. The output of the LSTM-AE constitutes the estimated dataset. Subsequently, ML/DL TSP models are trained and tested using the falsified, actual, and estimated versions of the dataset basically to demonstrate how the LSTM-AE-based mitigation strategy enhances the accuracy of the TSP models, reinstating its performance to levels achieved when tested and trained with the original, unfalsified dataset.

4.2 Proposed Method: LSTM-AE for Rectifying Falsified PMU Data

In this section, a detailed description of the input requirements is provided, along with an in-depth look at the architecture of the LSTM-AE model, which is designed to counter the detrimental effects of FDI. As depicted in Fig. 2, after the PMU measures the phasors of the analog voltage (or current) signal, these phasors are transmitted via a WAN for various controlling and monitoring tasks. Following the modification of PMU data through the vulnerabilities of transmission protocols, which are not the main focus of this study, and the injection of false data, the direct use of these measurements in a TSP model results in highly inaccurate predictions, as will be demonstrated in Sect. 4.4. Thus, to address this issue, we employ a mitigation and correction approach by initially feeding the altered measurements into an LSTM-AE. The input to our model is represented as

$$x^t = \{f^t_{PMU_1}, |u|^t_{PMU_1}, \angle u^t_{PMU_1}, \ldots, f^t_{PMU_N}, |u|^t_{PMU_N}, \angle u^t_{PMU_N}\} \tag{12}$$

where N is the total number of PMUs, equal to 10 in our case. In the preprocessing phase, these measurements are normalized using z-score normalization, adjusting the mean to zero and standard deviation to one. This normalization is crucial for optimizing data processing in LSTM units, enhancing their ability to identify patterns and dependencies.

Upon establishing the dimensional parameters of the input dataset, the structural design of the LSTM network is meticulously devised. The encoder part of the LSTM network comprises a layer with 10×3 units, followed by a subsequent layer containing 10 units. Conversely, the LSTM decoder is structured with an initial layer of 10 units, followed by a layer of 10×3 units. The training regimen for the LSTM network extends over 1,000 epochs. It incorporates an L2 regularization factor set at 0.0001 and employs a learning rate of 0.001. The optimization of the LSTM model is facilitated using the root mean squared error (RMSE) as the loss function, calculated as the square root of the average squared differences between the predicted/estimated values ($\tilde{x}^t = \{\tilde{f}_{PMU_1}^t, |\tilde{u}|_{PMU_1}^t, \angle \tilde{u}_{PMU_1}^t, \ldots, \tilde{f}_{PMU_N}^t, |\tilde{u}|_{PMU_N}^t, \angle \tilde{u}_{PMU_N}^t\}$) and actual values ($x^t$). Mathematically, this is represented as:

$$RMSE = \sqrt{\frac{1}{T} \sum_{t=1}^{T} (x^t - \tilde{x}^t)^2} \tag{13}$$

where T denotes the total number of observations.

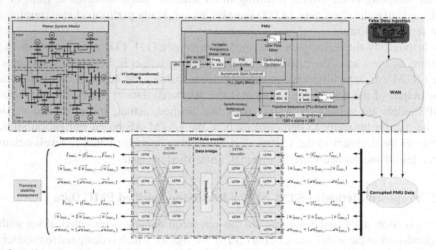

Fig. 2. Mitigating false data for accurate data-Driven-based TSP: A comprehensive overview of the proposed LSTM-AE model.

For the optimization process, the study employs the Adam optimization algorithm, a stochastic gradient-based method known for its efficiency in handling large datasets and non-stationary objectives. The computational experiments are executed on a high-performance computing setup, specifically on an Intel Core i7 CPU operating at 3.2 GHz, complemented by 16 GB of RAM.

4.3 Model Performance Evaluation

To rigorously ascertain the effectiveness of the developed LSTM-AE network, a validation procedure was conducted using a selected test dataset. Figure 3 exemplifies a comparative analysis encompassing three distinct sets of electrical parameters: voltage frequency (as depicted in Fig. 3a), voltage angle (illustrated in Fig. 3b), and voltage magnitude (presented in Fig. 3c). This figure methodically contrasts the actual measurements with those subjected to deliberate perturbation via FDI attacks, alongside the estimations obtained from the LSTM-AE model. The efficacy of the LSTM-AE in accurately tracking and estimating the frequency is evident in these illustrations. This is further clarified in Table 1, where the performance metrics are quantitatively presented. The metrics include:

- Aggregated and maximum RMSE are determined in accordance with (13).
- Mean absolute percentage error (MAPE), calculated as follows:

$$MAPE = \left(\frac{100}{T}\right) \sum_{t-1}^{T} \left|\frac{x^t - \tilde{x}^t}{x^t}\right| \qquad (14)$$

- Absolute percentage error (APE), defined as:

$$APE = (100) \left|\frac{x^t - \tilde{x}^t}{x^t}\right| \qquad (15)$$

Given the results, which show LSTM-AE's superior performance in accurately tracking and estimating frequency compared to its ability in angle and magnitude estimation, frequency has been selected as the focus variable for the TSP task in the subsequent section.

Table 1. Validation performance.

Variable	Performance			
	RMSE (agg.)	RMSE (max.)	MAPE	APE (max.)
Frequency	0.059	0.009	0.00020	0.00199
Angle	0.120	0.021	0.04768	1.0547
Magnitude	0.292	0.043	0.07540	1.5567

4.4 Impact on ML/DL-Based TSA Models

In the pursuit of the principal objective elucidated in this research, which seeks to enhance the precision of TSA through the utilization of LSTM-AE in the presence of FDI attacks for the rectification of falsified measurements, our approach entails a comprehensive evaluation of ML-based TSP models employing three distinct datasets: actual data, falsified data (corrupted data resulting from FDI), and estimated data.

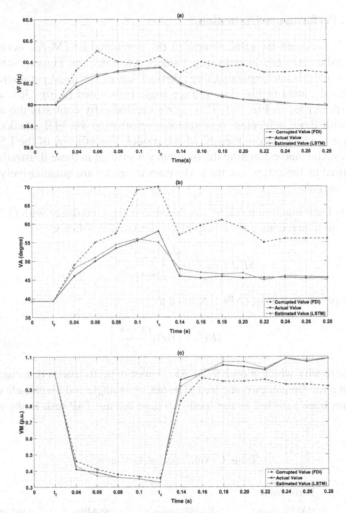

Fig. 3. Correction efficacy of LSTM-AE model for (a) Voltage Frequency, (b) Voltage Angle, and (c) Voltage Magnitude, in the presence of FDI attacks.

Benchmark algorithms, as delineated in [20], serve as the foundation for our evaluation. The comparative results of this analysis are succinctly encapsulated in Table 2. A critical observation from our findings is the convergence of the TSP accuracy towards the level attained with actual (unfalsified) data when the LSTM-AE algorithm is employed to correct and mitigate the effects of the FDI attack. Conversely, the accuracy of the models markedly deteriorates when the falsified data remains unmitigated.

Table 2. TSP performance.

Dataset	Algorithm	Accuracy	F1-Score
Actual Data	LightGBM	0.996	0.998
	LSTM	0.988	0.992
	MLP	0.990	0.994
	SVM	0.989	0.992
	Random Forest	0.997	0.998
	KNN	0.996	0.998
Falsified Data	LightGBM	0.746	0.833
	LSTM	0.759	0.837
	MLP	0.723	0.814
	SVM	0.764	0.855
	Random Forest	0.787	0.879
	KNN	0.701	0.804
Estimated Data (with LSTM-AE)	LightGBM	0.983	0.990
	LSTM	0.972	0.988
	MLP	0.961	0.985
	SVM	0.976	0.989
	Random Forest	0.986	0.991
	KNN	0.985	0.991

5   Conclusion

This article proposed a spatiotemporal learning model, employing LSTM-AE, to effectively learn the underlying normative spatial and temporal correlation patterns that are manifest in the dynamics of PMU data, encompassing both steady-state and transient operational conditions. The primary goal was to correct data distorted by FDI attacks through reconstruction, and then enhance the accuracy of ML-based TSP models by feeding them this rectified data. The strength of the proposed LSTM-AE model was highlighted in its capacity to reconstruct falsified PMU measurements, thereby effectively mitigating the adversarial impacts posed by FDI attacks. A noteworthy feature of our model's performance lies in its enhanced accuracy in tracking and estimating frequency, a critical parameter for accurate TSP. Comparative analysis with established ML-based TSP algorithms substantiates the augmented efficacy of our proposed model in scenarios involving FDI attacks. Subsequent investigations may aim to broaden the scope of the model's expertise, not only in accurately correcting falsified frequency measurements but also in precisely calibrating additional parameters such as magnitude and angle, which are critical metrics measured by PMUs. The anticipated advancement of this model is expected to yield a more robust and precise TSP in the context of FDI attack scenarios, thereby enhancing the resilience and reliability of power systems in the face of such cyber threats.

References

1. Muir, A., Lopatto, J.: Final report on the August 14, 2003 blackout in the United States and Canada: causes and recommendations (2004)
2. Makarov, Y.V., Reshetov, V.I., Stroev, A., Voropai, I.: Blackout prevention in the United States, Europe, and Russia. Proc. IEEE **93**, 1942–1955 (2005)
3. Behdadnia, T., Yaslan, Y., Genc, I.: A new method of decision tree based transient stability assessment using hybrid simulation for real-time PMU measurements. IET Gener. Transm. Distrib. **15**, 678–693 (2020)
4. Xie, J., Sun, W.: A transfer and deep learning-based method for online frequency stability assessment and Control. IEEE Access **9**, 75712–75721 (2021)
5. Chen, Q., Lin, N., Bu, S., Wang, H., Zhang, B.: Interpretable time-adaptive transient stability assessment based on dual-stage attention mechanism. IEEE Trans. Power Syst. **38**, 2776–2790 (2023)
6. Behdadnia, T., Parlak, M.: EV-integrated power system transient stability prediction based on imaging time series and Deep Neural Network. In: 2021 IEEE International Intelligent Transportation Systems Conference (ITSC) (2021)
7. Siamak, S., Dehghani, M., Mohammadi, M.: Dynamic GPS spoofing attack detection, localization, and measurement correction exploiting PMU and SCADA. IEEE Syst. J. **15**, 2531–2540 (2021)
8. Reda, H.T., Anwar, A., Mahmood, A.: Comprehensive survey and taxonomies of false data injection attacks in smart grids: attack models, targets, and impacts. Renew. Sustain. Energy Rev. **163**, 112423 (2022)
9. Behdadnia, T., Deconinck, G.: A new deep learning-based strategy for launching timely DOS attacks in PMU-based Cyber-Physical Power Systems. In: 2022 IEEE PES Innovative Smart Grid Technologies Conference Europe (ISGT-Europe) (2022)
10. Behdadnia, T., Thoelen, K., Zobiri, F., Deconinck, G.: Leveraging deep learning to increase the success rate of DOS attacks in PMU-based automatic generation control systems. IEEE Trans. Ind. Inform., 1–14 (2024). https://doi.org/10.1109/TII.2023.3342413
11. Zhang, J., Chu, Z., Sankar, L., Kosut, O.: False data injection attacks on phasor measurements that bypass low-rank decomposition. In: 2017 IEEE International Conference on Smart Grid Communications (SmartGridComm) (2017)
12. Chu, Z., Zhang, J., Kosut, O., Sankar, L.: Unobservable false data injection attacks against pmus: feasible conditions and multiplicative attacks. In: 2018 IEEE International Conference on Communications, Control, and Computing Technologies for Smart Grids (SmartGridComm) (2018)
13. Alexopoulos, T.A., Korres, G.N., Manousakis, N.M.: Complementarity reformulations for false data injection attacks on PMU-only state estimation. Electric Power Syst. Res. **189**, 106796 (2020)
14. Chu, Z., Zhang, J., Kosut, O., Sankar, L.: N-1 reliability makes it difficult for false data injection attacks to cause physical consequences. IEEE Trans. Power Syst. **36**, 3897–3906 (2021)
15. Almasabi, S., et al.: A novel technique to detect false data injection attacks on phasor measurement units. Sensors **21**, 5791 (2021)
16. Almasabi, S., et al.: False data injection detection for phasor measurement units. Sensors **22**, 3146 (2022)

17. Khare, G., Mohapatra, A., Singh, S.N.: A real-time approach for detection and correction of false data in PMU measurements. Electr. Power Syst. Res. **191**, 106866 (2021)
18. Pai, M.A.: Energy Function Analysis for Power System Stability. Kluwer Academic Publishers, Boston (1989)
19. DSATools Dynamic Security Assessment Software. http://www.dsatools.com. Accessed 25 Jan 2024
20. Aygul, K., Mohammadpourfard, M., Kesici, M., Kucuktezcan, F., Genc, I.: Benchmark of machine learning algorithms on transient stability prediction in renewable rich power grids under cyber-attacks. Internet Things **25**, 101012 (2024)

Legal Framework on Trustworthy Artificial Intelligence and Blockchain Technology Application

Iryna Sofinska[✉] [iD]

Lviv Polytechnic National University, Lviv 79005, Ukraine
iryna.d.sofinska@lpnu.ua

Abstract. Faced with the prompt technological development of AI and blockchain technologies globally, policymakers are empowered to propose (make) laws to protect fundamental human rights following the opportunities and addressing challenges, even threats, presented by AI applications in everyday life. It aims to set future-proof and innovation-friendly standards, draft legal frameworks, develop new global norms, and harmonize landmark rules to ensure AI can be trusted: it is a force for good in society, works for people, and is not considered a clear threat to them. Democracy, the rule of law, safety and security, transparency, and trust following the protection of fundamental human rights are at stake. AI that help to manipulate human behavior to circumvent users' free will and permit some 'social scoring' by governments or pro-government majority in the parliament should be banned while demonstrating potential danger, clear threat, and causing unacceptable risk. Several countries worldwide (Australia, Brazil, Canada, China, India, Japan, Korea, New Zealand, Saudi Arabia, Singapore, the United Kingdom, and the USA) have adopted a proactive approach toward AI regulation. Those countries aim to implement essential policies and infrastructure measures to cultivate a robust AI sector rather than introduce specific legislation to regulate its growth. Without comprehensive legislation, governments have published some legal frameworks, guidelines, and roadmaps, white papers that depict the future of possible AI regulation in these countries and help responsibly manage their AI usage. Finally, the European Union joined 'the club' following the political agreement reached recently, on December 11, 2023, between the European Parliament and the Council on the Artificial Intelligence Act (the first-ever comprehensive legal framework on AI globally), proposed by the Commission in April 2021.

Keywords: trust · AI · blockchain technologies

1 Introduction

AI blockchain technology should be based on trust and used wisely and widely to guarantee the safety of fundamental human rights and the security of governments (and municipalities) or companies and foster responsible innovation. People want to apply AI for general purposes, benefit from a free pass, 'smart city' toolkit, and energy sustainability, use spam filters, and employ chatbots. Still, real-time remote biometric identification

B. Sangchoolie et al. (Eds.): EDCC 2024 Workshops, CCIS 2078, pp. 104–107, 2024.
https://doi.org/10.1007/978-3-031-56776-6_10

for law enforcement purposes in publicly accessible spaces, categorization, and emotion recognition systems (i.e., in the workplace) are at high risk following fundamental human rights protection (while AI application, in some cases, is manipulative, a clear threat, and potential danger encouraging dangerous behavior of minors). Also, deep fakes, misinformation, and other AI-generated content are often used to gain power and win parliamentary or presidential elections.

We try to define those segments where AI and blockchain technology applications might threaten the lives and put the health of citizens at risk (even potential danger): transport and other specific critical infrastructures (i.e., in the fields of water, gas, and electricity); medical devices (AI applications in robot-assisted surgery); systems to determine access to educational institutions or for recruiting people (scoring of exams and CV-sorting software for recruitment procedures); law enforcement and evaluation of the reliability of evidence; border control and verification of the authenticity of travel documents and identification of (in and out-of-country) travelers; credit scoring which denies citizens the opportunity to obtain a necessary loan; administration of justice and democratic processes (voting process), etc.

This research bridges technologies, science, law, and politics at a crossroads between digitalization, innovation, transparency, sustainability, and human dignity by facilitating and enhancing cooperation on AI and BCT applications.

2 Methodology

Apart from general scientific research methods (like analysis, synthesis, analogy, generalization, and prognosis), we use other specific methods (data analysis, statistical, comparative) to emphasize AI's origin, development, and influence on everyday life. All these methods help to depict the necessity of drafting a legal framework (even hypothetical constitutional amending) for AI-generated and blockchain technology applications.

Comparative and legal approaches focus on identifying a four-tiered risk approach (limited, minimal, high, unacceptable) that should be defined by legislation (not only on international and supranational levels but also on national, constitutional, regional, and local levels). For example, the recently agreed EU AI Act still possesses some extensive top-down prescriptive rules regarding risk-related approaches [1]. Even some EU member-states want to liberalize the use of facial recognition by their police forces. On the contrary, the United States is taking its typical decentralized approach [2]; however, they will unlikely pass a broad national AI law (successful and less controversial legal framework) over the next few years.

3 Findings

AI development is a competitive advantage for every country [3]. Public sector officials, companies, and civic society should continue jump-started conversations about the uses of AI and how to govern it to understand better the evolving regulatory landscape of AI and blockchain technology applications to strike the right balance between government oversight, policymaking, and innovation [4].

In the international arena, core principles for AI application are defined by the OECD and endorsed by the G20, following the respect for fundamental human rights, sustainability, transparency, the rule of law, robust risk-based management, privacy, non-discrimination, safety, security, and policy clarity [5] (Table 1).

Table 1.

OECD AI principles	OECD recommendations to governments
AI should benefit people and the planet by driving inclusive growth, sustainable development, and well-being	Facilitate public and private investment in research and development to spur innovation in trustworthy AI
AI systems should be designed to respect the rule of law, human rights, democratic values, and diversity, and they should include appropriate safeguards – for example, enabling human intervention where necessary – to ensure a fair and just society	Foster accessible AI ecosystems with digital infrastructure, technologies, and mechanisms to share data and knowledge
There should be transparency and responsible disclosure around AI systems to ensure that people understand when they are engaging with them and that they can challenge outcomes	Create a policy environment that will open the way to deploying trustworthy AI systems
AI systems must function robustly, securely, and safely throughout their lifetimes, and potential risks should be continually assessed and managed	Equip people with the skills for AI and support workers to ensure a fair transition
Organizations and individuals developing, deploying, or operating AI systems should be held accountable for their proper functioning per the above principles	Co-operate across borders and sectors to share information, develop standards, and work toward responsible stewardship of AI
OECD AI principles	OECD recommendations to governments
AI should benefit people and the planet by driving inclusive growth, sustainable development, and well-being	Facilitate public and private investment in research and development to spur innovation in trustworthy AI

G7 leaders agreed recently, on October 30, 2023, on International Guiding Principles on Artificial Intelligence (AI) and a voluntary Code of Conduct for AI developers under the Hiroshima AI process. We can enlist a few critical parameters of successful AI regulatory design (adaptive and outcome-based, risk-weight, collaborative regulation, regulatory sandboxes), challenged by the existential question - how do we balance innovation and societal risks (i.e., safety, bias, transparency, privacy, (cyber)security, trust, copyright, content regulation, education, and productivity)?

4   Conclusions

AI blockchain technology applications are developing and transforming diverse industries, reshaping the world (i.e., enabling 'smart city' management and delivering better service to citizens at lower cost to taxpayers). AI platforms can reinforce and perpetuate centurial human biases (based on gender, race, religion, ethnic origin, or sexual orientation), undermine personal rights, compromise data security and confidentiality, produce misinformation, deep fakes, and disinformation, destabilize the financial system and mobile service and cause other forms of mass disruption worldwide. This 'tailor-made' approach to the AI regulation framework (national rulemaking) should consider other digital policy priorities such as cybersecurity, data privacy, and intellectual property protection. Policymakers should consider a regulatory framework for AI-generated systems application (based on risk and unintended consequences), which includes areas related to bias of algorithm and copyrights (a few already targeted issues are intellectual property and cybersecurity), and pass new relevant, resilient, transparent, and equitable legislation to maximize AI's benefits to society while mitigating its risks, respond to public concerns about AI and blockchain technology applications. From a short-term perspective, policymakers globally, to the extent possible, should develop a certain set of rules that meet the core objective of promoting safe, secure, and ethical AI while considering the implications of recent higher-risk innovation associated with AI and blockchain technology where closer oversight may be appropriate.

Acknowledgments. This project has received funding from the European Union's Horizon 2020 research and innovation programme under the Marie Skłodowska-Curie grant agreement No 101007820. This publication reflects only the author's view and the REA is not responsible for any use that may be made of the information it contains.

Disclosure of Interests.   The authors have no competing interests to declare that are relevant to the content of this article.

References

1. Artificial Intelligence Act (AIA) (2023). https://eur-lex.europa.eu/legal-content/EN/TXT/?qid=1623335154975&uri=CELEX-%3A52021PC0206
2. Blueprint for an AI Bill of Rights (2022). http://www.whitehouse.gov/ostp/ai-bill-of-rights
3. Establishing a pro-innovation approach to regulating AI (2022). https://www.gov.uk/government/publications/establishing-a-pro-innovation-approach-to-regulating-ai
4. Provisions on the Administration of Algorithm Recommendation of Internet Information Services in China (2022). http://www.gov.cn/zhengce/zhengceku/2022-01/04/content_5666429.htm
5. Organization for Economic Co-operation and Development (OECD AI) Principles (2019). https://oecd.ai/en/ai-principles

An Exploratory Study on Trust in Blockchain-Enabled Energy Trading

Niccolò Testi [✉] [iD]

University of Macerata, Piaggia dell'Università, 2, 62100 Macerata, MC, Italy
n.testi@unimc.it

Abstract. This exploratory study investigates the relationship between trust and blockchain technology (BCT) in peer-to-peer (P2P) energy trading within smart grids. The research highlights the various benefits BCT brings to P2P energy trading, such as improved efficiency, cost reduction, and the optimization of renewable energy distribution. However, it also identifies significant barriers to the contribution of BCT to the removal of trust in this context. The paper explores how trust is established in blockchain systems and the paradoxical need for trust among parties for BCT adoption in energy trading, despite its trust-removing premise, due to its reliance on oracles for data collection. It also examines the blockchain trilemma and how solutions to the lack of scalability might reintroduce centralisation, affecting trust in BCT-enabled P2P energy trading. The study suggests that BCT may not be able to remove the need for trust and trusted intermediaries in P2P energy trading and calls for more qualitative research to assess the actual impact of BCT on trust in P2P energy trading and to compare traditional and blockchain-based systems in this domain.

Keywords: Blockchain · Energy Trading · Trust

1 Introduction

Smart grids represent an evolution in electricity network technology, integrating advanced communication and data analytics capabilities to manage electricity flow more efficiently and responsively [1]. This grid system supports the integration of various energy sources, including renewable energies like solar and wind, and facilitates improved grid management and reliability [2]. Energy trading, within this context, becomes more dynamic and sophisticated. It involves the buying and selling of electricity, often in real-time, based on fluctuating supply and demand [3]. The data-driven insights provided by smart grids enable more accurate forecasting and pricing strategies in energy trading [4]. This synergy enhances market efficiency, allows for more effective balancing of energy supply with consumer demand, and encourages the adoption of renewable energy sources by enabling the sale of surplus energy generated by these sources [5]. Smart grids and energy trading together facilitate the transition towards a more sustainable, flexible, and resilient energy ecosystem [3].

B. Sangchoolie et al. (Eds.): EDCC 2024 Workshops, CCIS 2078, pp. 108–122, 2024.
https://doi.org/10.1007/978-3-031-56776-6_11

Blockchain technology (BCT), primarily known for its role in cryptocurrencies, is now being adapted to foster decentralized smart grids and enable peer-to-peer (P2P) energy trading [6]. Centralized energy grids, characterized by long-distance energy transmissions, are plagued with issues like significant energy loss and low fault tolerance. In contrast, decentralized smart grids leverage distributed energy resources, such as solar panels and windmills, which generate power locally, thereby mitigating these issues. However, their integration into the energy market necessitates a reliable platform for energy trading, which is where BCT comes into play [7]. BCT enables secure and transparent P2P energy trading, allowing for the direct exchange of surplus electricity between parties, and tracking transactions with its distributed ledger system. This system not only simplifies the trading process but also enables consumers to make informed choices about their energy sources, potentially reducing costs by eliminating intermediaries [8]. In renewable energy, particularly solar, blockchain can optimize the distribution of surplus energy, addressing the intermittency issues of renewables [9]. Given the numerous benefits that BCT is supposed to bring to P2P energy trading, it is not surprising that academic interest in the topic has been growing throughout the years [10].

However, some barriers may hinder the diffusion of BCT for P2P energy trading [11]. First, as in all non-crypto applications of BCT, data that is notarised on the blockchain needs to be collected and provided by oracles, placed in the real world, which must be trusted with the collection of correct data. Secondly, potential sources of lack of trust come from the technical aspects of the blockchain used for energy trading. Blockchain-based P2P energy trading systems face potential scalability issues which call for a reflection on the trade-offs between efficiency and decentralization [12]. Indeed, solutions to the lack of scalability involve using certain consensus algorithms like Proof of Stake (PoS) [13] and Proof of Authority PoA [14], permissioned blockchain architecture (mainly of the consortium type) [15], and off-chain transactions [16, 17]. However, all these solutions reintroduce centralisation in a system that is trusted because of its decentralisation bringing security and immutability to the ledger, thus, the solutions may hinder trust in BCT-enabled P2P energy trading.

This study explores the relationship between BCT-enabled energy trading and trust, suggesting future research studies to deepen the understanding on the usefulness of this technology for energy trading and benchmark it with other solutions based on other technologies.

2 The Oracle Problem in Blockchain-Enabled Energy Trading

Trust is an essential psychological foundation for cooperation where uncertainty and risk characterize interpersonal relationships [18]. When a trusting individual takes a risk, they make themselves vulnerable, believing that the other party will act beneficially. The trustor lacks control over the trustee's actions, creating a degree of uncertainty [19]. This trust is a vital component for economic transactions to take place; without it, transactions become virtually impossible [20]. As trust minimizes transaction costs and facilitates new forms of cooperation and business advancement [21], its absence can impede economic growth [22]. With an increasing number of transactions happening digitally, trust becomes even more critical. However, the centralization of user data in singular databases controlled by a single entity raises issues. This model is technically and governance-wise centralized, leading to an increasing distrust among individuals towards these data-holding organizations, mainly due to their lack of transparency in information sharing [23] which is crucial in inter-organizational digital collaborations [24]. As a result, decentralized networks such as blockchains are seen as a natural progression, where trust shifts from centralised systems controlled by banks or states to algorithms and encryption software [25].

Blockchains allow trust in the system's outcome without needing to trust individual participants [26]. This is achieved through the blockchains' consensus protocol, which is a set of rules and processes that allows all the nodes of the blockchain network to agree on the validity of transactions and the current state of the distributed ledger; this agreement is crucial in a decentralized system where there is no central authority to dictate or validate the state of the ledger [27]. This ensures that participants have faith in their ledgers' accuracy and consistency [28]. Further, cryptographic techniques solve problems such as double-spending, which refers to the illicit act of spending the same digital currency twice, exploiting vulnerabilities in the ledger, and the challenge of achieving consensus in distributed systems with unreliable components [29]. Consequently, actors place trust in the technology rather than the involved parties [30, 31]. With blockchain, algorithmic trust replaces traditional interpersonal trust, representing a paradigm shift from trusting people to trusting mathematics [32, 33]. Also, there is no need to trust intermediaries [34], as cryptographic consensus and transparency allow everyone to operate with less need for trust in institutions [35].

As Chowdhury et al. (2018) state, a deficit of trust among parties is the most important requirement for choosing to use blockchains rather than centralized databases to exchange data. Blockchains are preferable to centralised databases when multiple parties wanting to share data between them do not trust each other and cannot (or do not want to) find a trusted third party to ensure the correctness and immutable storage of such data. Indeed, Sternberg et al. (2020) theorize that if trust between parties is already present, then the adoption of BCT would not create more trust and is ultimately unnecessary.

The features of predictability, reliability, and transparency of the blockchain protocol establish the blockchain as a trust-free technology [38, 39]; in other words, BCT removes the need for trust in the P2P exchange of value, because peers can rely on the predictable and reliable functioning of the blockchain protocol itself. The blockchain, often termed as a trust-less system or a trust machine, can be seen as the basis for a truly trust-free economy [40] for its capacity to create a secure, publicly accessible record of past transactions agreed upon by all, removing trust issues in P2P exchange of value [41].

The term "value", in the context of BCT, is not limited to the monetary value itself, represented by the cryptocurrency, instead, the value for blockchains' users is the possibility to exchange cryptocurrency safely and transparently without intermediaries. In this sense, the value is the metadata about the transactions (i.e., the addresses of the peers between which the transactions were made, the timestamps stating when the transactions were made, or the information about the block the transaction was closed into, and other relevant information) and the fact that such metadata are available to parties interested in them. Parties can trust the metadata of the transactions because it is generated by the blockchain protocol.

In other cases, BCT is not used to exchange cryptocurrency P2P but is used to store data collected from the outside world and not generated by the blockchain protocol. This data is relevant to someone, for whom the value is also the metadata associated with the transactions that contain the data. For example, transactions can contain energy trading data that are valuable for authorities and consumers, who want to check the metadata to know who put the data on the blockchain, when, in which block, etc. In this case, while the parties can trust the metadata created by the blockchain protocol, they cannot be sure about the truthfulness of the data stored inside the transactions [42]. Indeed, the data are provided by oracles placed in the real world – oracles that could lie or malfunction and provide incorrect data [43]. Continuing with the example of storing energy trading data in blockchain transactions, the parties that are interested in this data cannot know if the data, collected by oracles which could be people or machines, correctly represents what occurred [44]. On the one hand, theoretically, blockchains' transparency and immutability should discourage parties from any misconduct (e.g., uploading false or inaccurate data to the blockchain) [45], on the other hand, blockchains cannot eliminate the risk of fraudulent behaviour [44] and trust must be placed in the oracles providing the data [43]. This creates a situation, individuated by Sternberg et al. (2020), where parties want to adopt BCT to remove the need for trust in the exchange of data among them, but since they cannot be sure of the correctness of the data they provide to each other through the blockchain, they need to know and trust each other before adopting BCT. This means that trust among parties is a prerequisite for BCT adoption. This leads to a paradox: if trust among parties is already present, then the adoption of BCT to remove the need for trust is not necessary [37]. Likewise, it can be argued that if a deficit of trust among parties was the reason for their will to adopt BCT, then BCT would not help solve it. Otherwise, as A. Zhang et al. (2020) noted, if parties cannot trust each other with the data they provide to each other in the blockchain network, then the only solution would be to involve trusted third parties to ensure that the data are correct, nevertheless, this would reintroduce intermediaries where they were meant to be removed. It is not surprising, then, that there is scepticism that BCT will be able to remove the need for trust and intermediaries in non-crypto applications [43] like energy trading.

3 Solving Blockchain's Limited Scalability at the Expense of Trust

The lack of scalability in blockchains is a problem if there is the need to store huge amounts of data in them in a short time [47, 48]. To accommodate the need for higher scalability, some solutions have been proposed, such as fragmenting a ledger into sub-ledgers, removing old transactions, and using multiple blockchains on different levels [49]; however, the solutions studied, proposed, and applied the most are off-chain storage, the use of specific consensus algorithms in blockchains, and the creation of permissioned blockchain networks with private or consortium architectures.

As will be explained in the following paragraphs, due to the blockchain trilemma, all these solutions enable more scalability at the expense of decentralization and security. Since decentralization and security are positively linked to parties' trust [36, 50], these solutions, when implemented in blockchains, may have the effect of decreasing trust among blockchains' parties.

3.1   The Blockchain Trilemma

Centralised databases are usually siloed, i.e., not visible to parties interested in accessing the data they contain, and the data stored in them can easily be changed or eliminated by the database owner(s) or hackers [36]. Instead, blockchains are immutable and usually accessible databases that enable P2P transactions without the intermediation of trusted third parties (Attaran and Gunasekaran, 2019; Bodkhe *et al.*, 2020). Also, blockchains are more secure than centralised databases because the ledger containing the transactions is copied in all the nodes of the blockchain network, thus eliminating the problem of the single point of failure caused by the single node's malfunctioning or hacking [36, 50].

However, this technical feature also requires that new information is distributed to all the nodes of the network before any other additional information can be written in the database, making blockchains not as scalable as centralised databases [53]. The limited scalability issue happens when the number of transactions to be validated goes beyond a certain threshold. The bandwidth needed to process the increasing volume of transactions will get higher [54], leading to an increase in the time required to validate transactions [55]. The validation time can be related to various factors: network delay, consensus delay among multiple orders, execution time, endorsement delay, and block validation delay [54]. It can also be related to the amount of data processed with every transaction. Transactions that involve heavy files (e.g., images and videos) require a higher amount of bandwidth to maintain a sustainable transaction throughput speed, even with a good Internet connection [55]. This means that it is impossible to store huge amounts of data in a short time in blockchains [56], making it not feasible to use blockchain to store heavy files like digital documents, pictures, or videos [57] unless the number of nodes is greatly decreased, in which case the blockchain's decentralisation and security is hindered [58]: this is the "blockchain trilemma".

The blockchain trilemma, as explained by Reno & Haque (2023), refers to the challenge of simultaneously achieving three critical aspects of a blockchain ledger: security, scalability, and decentralization. Balancing these factors is complex because enhancing one or two of them often negatively impacts the others. For instance, increasing scalability can compromise security, and prioritizing security and scalability can hinder decentralization. Adding nodes that store the ledger to the network increases decentralisation, and this increases resilience against attacks and improves integrity and availability [60]; but, since these nodes perform redundant computation and data storage across the network, increasing their number also increases the overall cost of operating the blockchain [61]. On the contrary, having more scalability means either having fewer nodes or using more centralised consensus algorithms, thus diminishing decentralisation and security [59] and, consequently, trust among parties of the blockchain network.

3.2   Off-Chain Storage

Off-chain storage has been proposed as a solution to the low scalability of blockchains [57, 59]. Using off-chain storage means that the data are not uploaded on-chain, i.e., to the blockchain, but off-chain, i.e., on a centralised database, while only the hash derived from the data is stored on-chain for immutable reference [62]. Hashing is a process where an algorithm, known as a hash function, converts any content it is given as input into an output that is a fixed-size string of bytes, typically a sequence of numbers and letters, called hash, which univocally identifies that content [63]. Since all hashes have the same size independently of the data they are derived from and weigh all the same limited amount of bytes, uploading only the hashes to a blockchain mitigates the on-chain storage scalability problem because it decreases the size of the data exchanged on-chain between the nodes and, consequently, lowers the time that it takes for the data to be broadcasted to the whole network before another block can be added to the blockchain, which makes the blockchain more scalable [57]. In sum, with off-chain storage, data are stored in a centralised database, while the data's hashes are stored in the blockchain for reference. A stakeholder having access to both a file on the centralised database and its immutable hash on the blockchain can see if the hash calculated from the file at that moment is the same as the one put on the blockchain previously. If the two hashes coincide, then the file's content has not been modified [64].

But, as noted by Hepp et al. (2018), a fundamental flaw of off-chain storage is the risk of loss of data or the impossibility of accessing the data. This could happen because of a malfunction of the centralised database, which is a single point of failure. To mitigate this risk, some researchers have proposed that data manager(s) store the data off-chain in decentralised networks such as IPFS that allow replication of data on multiple nodes [64, 65]; nevertheless, the data are still under the control of the data manager(s) who could arbitrarily decide to eliminate the data or make them unreachable to parties. Indeed, [57] say that off-chain storage might not always align with the principle of decentralization and data transparency, leading to potential trust issues among parties. Chowdhury et al. (2018) state that if data durability is a requirement, then on-chain storage must be used.

3.3 PoS and PoA Consensus Algorithms

A consensus algorithm in blockchain is a set of rules and processes that allows all the participants of the blockchain network to agree on the validity of transactions and the current state of the distributed ledger; this agreement is crucial in a decentralized system where there is no central authority to dictate or validate the state of the ledger [27]. Many consensus algorithms exist, each one with its characteristics [66, 67], but for the scope of explaining the impact of consensus algorithms on scalability and trust, only the three most studied and used ones will be considered: Proof-of-Work (PoW), Proof-of-Stake (PoS), and Proof-of-Authority (POA).

PoW is the original consensus algorithm, used by the Bitcoin Blockchain. Miners, who are usually anonymous and do not need permission to have this role, compete to solve complex cryptographic puzzles to create new blocks; the first to solve the puzzle gets to add the new block of transactions to the blockchain. The process is costly because it requires significant computational power, meaning that miners need to have powerful hardware, use lots of electricity, and spend much time trying to solve the puzzle, but precisely for this reason, it is extremely difficult and anti-economic to conduct a 51% attack to change the data in a block. Also, since all miners are competing to create the same block and it takes a long time to create it, PoW does not allow for a high transaction throughput, which makes the blockchains using it not scalable. The PoS consensus algorithm, used in the Ethereum Blockchain, was invented to solve the problem of the high electricity consumption of PoW [66]. In PoS, participants express their willingness to be part of the block creation process by locking a specified amount of their cryptocurrency in an escrow account. If they lock enough cryptocurrency, they gain the right to become "validators", which have the same role as the miners in the PoW and are similarly anonymous. The higher the stake, the greater the chance of being chosen to create the next block; furthermore, miners can lose their stake if they are found to be acting against the protocol's rules. This stake acts as a form of security, ensuring that participants adhere to the protocol rules. PoS can lead to faster transaction processing and less electricity usage compared to PoW because miners are chosen beforehand to mine their blocks, allowing multiple miners to mine their own assigned block simultaneously with other miners' blocks and no time spent to solve a challenge. Despite allowing for more scalability, PoS make the blockchain network less decentralised and lower its security by enabling a few richer nodes to have consistently more probability to be chosen as miners [68], thus making the blockchain more vulnerable to 51% attacks [67, 69]. Finally, the consensus on the validity of transactions and the current state of the distributed ledger in PoA is not based on computational power as in PoW or cryptocurrency amounts as in PoS but on identity and reputation [67]. Nodes' identities are known and are added to the network after permission is granted by the network operator(s), which is(are) generally known and trusted within the network. Nodes become validators and earn mining rewards, incentivizing them to maintain their reputable position. Despite PoA reducing the need for mining and expensive computational operations, leading to higher scalability and little energy usage than most other consensus protocols [70], Ekparinya et al. (2019) found that PoA exposes blockchain networks to security issues, mainly because the validators are low in number and must be pre-approved by the trusted controller(s) of the blockchain, usually without a transparent on-chain election system.

The consensus algorithm plays a vital role in BCT in maintaining the system's security and efficiency. Generally, the consensus algorithms requiring more work to mine blocks and allowing a larger number of actors to become miners or validators enable more decentralisation and distribution of power among the nodes in the blockchain network, and so are more secure because are less vulnerable to 51% attacks but are more costly to operate because of the higher mining difficulty. So, PoW is more secure than PoS, which is in turn more secure than PoA. Each consensus algorithm has its own set of trade-offs, including factors like energy efficiency, security, and the potential for centralization or decentralization. The choice of which consensus algorithm to implement in a blockchain depends on the governance and efficiency requirements that the blockchain must have for the parties, who are the ones that benefit from writing and reading the data on the blockchain. As E. Tan et al. (2022) state, PoW may be more suitable to create systems where power among nodes is distributed and decentralisation of governance is considered more important than scalability by the parties. In this regard, PoS achieves less decentralisation but increases scalability. Andoni et al. (2019) warn that using PoS to achieve scalability in blockchain-enabled energy trading may compromise security and decentralization and have dire long-term implications. Finally, PoA provides a high level of efficiency at the cost of being more centralized and may be more suitable to semi-centralized systems where parties need to know and trust the validator nodes and when it is necessary to store data in the blockchain in larger amounts and with less cost.

3.4 Blockchain Architectures: Public, Private, Consortium

Different blockchain architectures have been invented to accommodate the needs not only for more scalability but also for more control over the block creation process and data privacy. Ownership and governance differentiate the architectures. The distinction is between "permissionless" and "permissioned" blockchains; permissionless blockchains have a "public" kind of architecture, while permissioned blockchains can have a "consortium" or "private" architecture.

Permissionless blockchains such as Bitcoin are fully decentralized, are owned by nobody, and allow any node in the blockchain network to write, validate, and read the information stored in them. Thus, governance in permissionless blockchains is completely decentralised, with powers being equally distributed among the nodes. All nodes are anonymous, ensuring their privacy. Since anonymity could increase moral hazard and, consequently, perceived risk, the transactions are recorded, made immutable, and visible to everyone, creating a trust-less environment where trust between nodes is not necessary to start transactions of value [49]. On the contrary, permissioned blockchains can be owned either by one or more owners who have full control of the blockchain's functioning and can set different levels of accessibility and writing and reading rights to nodes. Validators that add blocks are known to the owners and pre-approved by them to have this role [73]. Thus, their governance is semi-decentralised. Permissioned blockchains have some advantages and disadvantages compared to permissionless blockchains. First, they perform more efficiently in terms of transaction validation speed (i.e., they are more scalable) due to a faster validation process and a smaller number of validating nodes [74]. The average time of a transaction being validated can be milliseconds and this could even enable real-time readability of data as soon as they are uploaded to the permissioned blockchain [55]. Second, permissioned blockchains enable owners to restrict access to the data uploaded to the blockchain [75], protecting sensitive data that nodes want to share just with other selected nodes [76], making it ideal to share data with selected parties only [77]. Indeed, data visibility to the public in permissionless blockchains may not always be desirable for parties that value data confidentiality [78]. Third, as noted by Mirabelli & Solina (2020), should some actors begin to act maliciously, they can be quickly removed from the network by their owners; additionally, in permissioned blockchains, all nodes are known and accountable for their actions, so they might be incentivized to act ethically, contrarily to what happens in permissionless blockchains where every node is protected by anonymity. However, even full accountability does not eliminate the risk of fraudulent behaviour [44]. Lastly, permissioned blockchains can allow their validators to change or eliminate the data in the blockchain, which is not possible in permissionless blockchains. Indeed, data immutability, while being considered a good feature of blockchains might not always be desirable. For example, it could be necessary to change the information uploaded to a blockchain if it contains errors or to eliminate some data that is not necessary to keep on the blockchain anymore. If a track of these operations and who did them is stored on the blockchain, the process is transparent [74, 80].

Further on the discourse about blockchain architectures, permissionless blockchains have a public architecture with completely decentralised governance since nobody owns the blockchain and everyone can validate blocks and write and read transactions. Contrarily, permissioned blockchains can have private and consortium architectures. A private blockchain is owned by a single entity that has total top-down control overwrite and read rights and the validation process. The structure of a private blockchain might look decentralized if the data contained in it are distributed among multiple nodes, however, these are controlled by the owner of the blockchain or by other parties under its control – so, private blockchains are the same as centralized databases [74]. The owner of a private blockchain can unilaterally choose to restrict access to some information, not to write certain transactions, or to modify or remove them altogether, even if performing these actions would lead to reputational damage for the owner itself if caught [81]. The other kind of permissioned blockchains is the consortium ones. Consortium blockchains mitigate some of the risks of private blockchains by removing centralized control on the blockchain [74] since control is shared among multiple equally powered owners, instead of being centralized in the hands of a single entity. The owners decide who can become a node of the network and who must be kicked out, grant writing, validating, and reading rights to nodes [82]. Validators are often pre-determined at the genesis of the blockchain and are usually its original owners [81]. While being different in terms of the level of decentralization, both private and consortium blockchains share the advantages of a faster transaction throughput speed, compared to permissionless blockchains, and the possibility for the owners to amend the data already stored in the blockchain [74].

The scalability issue is relevant in permissionless blockchains, which can be accessed by an unlimited number of users, while it can be less relevant in permissioned blockchains where access is restricted to a limited number of users [78]. Nonetheless, higher scalability in blockchains is usually achieved at the cost of lower decentralisation and security [58]. Permissionless public blockchains are the most distributed and secure, but the least scalable; private and consortium blockchains are more scalable but sacrifice decentralisation and security [49, 66]. Consortium blockchains, which compromise between decentralisation, security, and scalability, can be less transparent than permissionless ones and fail to build the parties' trust. The owners of a consortium blockchain could collude among themselves to limit access to important traceability information that, if disclosed, could damage them. Also, since only they have the right to mine and validate the blocks, they could refuse to validate some transactions, or they could cancel or change pre-validated transactions by mining the block that contains them and the following blocks. If the governance rules of the consortium blockchain do not require unanimity to take these kinds of decisions, only a part of the validators must collude for fraudulent behaviours to occur. Surely the validators put their reputation at stake in front of all the other parties, and this should refrain them from misbehaving. Moreover, the actual risk of validators colluding is not proved by any empirical evidence (meaning that it has not happened yet, or that it happened but nobody noticed). However, the mere hypothetical possibility of this happening could be enough to invalidate the parties' trust in the validators. Consequently, a consortium BC would fail to build trust among parties.

Finally, E. Tan et al. (2022) warn about the possibility that the power relations of actors may alter an initially decentralised governance structure into a centralised one: if on-chain governance is controlled by a few major operators with significant control over mining resources or token holdings, a system initially designed to be decentralized could operate more like a semi-centralized or polycentric governance structure. This is what happened, for instance, to the Bitcoin Blockchain network, where a limited set of entities currently control the mining and, consequently, the decision-making [83]. Despite the notion of a decentralized network being democratic and egalitarian, it can obscure the power imbalance and differences among the nodes [25].

4 Conclusion

In a blockchain network, parties trust the deterministic outcomes of the blockchain proto-col, and the immutability of the transactions stored in the blockchain, causing a shift from interpersonal trust to trusting the mathematics behind the blockchain protocol. In this sense, blockchains remove the need for interpersonal trust between peers that exchange value between them and for intermediaries as trusted third parties. In recent years, there has been a growing interest in academia about BCT as a tool for enabling decentralised P2P energy trading, the idea being that it would solve the lack of transparency typical of centralised trading systems. The expectation placed upon BCT-enabled energy trading is that it will enable trust between parties by making energy trading transactions immutable and visible to parties without the intervention of a third party to store and validate them.

However, two issues arise in the case of blockchain-enabled energy trading, as in all non-crypto applications of BCT. First, the energy trading data that are stored on the blockchain come from oracles placed in the real world, which could lie or malfunction and provide incorrect data, so they must be trusted. Also, intermediaries as trusted third parties may still be necessary to check if the data are correct. Consequently, the blockchain cannot remove the need for trust, contrarily, since parties cannot trust each other as oracles, pre-existing trust is necessary for BCT adoption. This leads to the paradox of BCT being desirable to remove the need for trust and intermediaries between parties but necessitating pre-existing trust among them and intermediaries to be adopted; but if trust among parties is present, or trusted third parties can be individuated to check the correctness of the data exchanged between them, then adopting BCT is not useful anymore. Second, blockchains have low scalability, meaning that it is impossible to store large quantities of data in them. Some solutions have been proposed, such as using off-chain storage, specific consensus algorithms, and permissioned blockchains, but all these measures reintroduce centralisation in a blockchain system that was supposed to be decentralised to bring trust among parties.

In sum, the question is if BCT-enabled energy trading can fulfil the expectations of trust removal that have been placed on it; unfortunately, the lack of empirical studies makes the answer still unknown, however, some scepticism on the capacity of BCT to remove the need for trust among parties in these kinds of applications is understandable.

More qualitative research is needed to assess if BCT-enabled energy trading removes the need for trust among parties or if at least it mitigates trust issues. Future research should compare traditional P2P energy trading systems with those that integrate BCT. This would involve analysing the levels of trust required in each system, the incidence of fraud or disputes, and the overall efficiency and reliability of transactions. Additionally, it would be useful to conduct in-depth case studies of existing blockchain-based P2P energy trading platforms to analyse any challenges or successes in reducing the need for trust. Finally, data gathered from users of P2P energy trading platforms, both blockchain-based and traditional through surveys and interviews, could provide insights into perceived trustworthiness. These studies should ideally be longitudinal to observe how trust dynamics evolve in blockchain-based P2P energy systems and involve multidisciplinary teams, combining expertise in BCT, energy trading, sociology, and psychology, to comprehensively assess the impact of BCT on trust in P2P energy trading.

Acknowledgments. This project has received funding from the European Union's Horizon 2020 research and innovation programme under the Marie Skłodowska-Curie grant agreement No 101007820. This publication reflects only the author's view and the REA is not responsible for any use that may be made of the information it contains.

Disclosure of Interests. The authors have no conflict of interest to declare.

References

1. Zhang, Y., Huang, T., Bompard, E.F.: Big data analytics in smart grids: a review. Energy Inform. **1**(1), 8 (2018). https://doi.org/10.1186/s42162-018-0007-5
2. Adebanji, B., Ojo, A., Fasina, T., Adeleye, S., Abere, J.: Integration of renewable energy with smart grid application into the Nigeria's power network: issues, challenges and opportunities. EJENG **7**(3), 18–24 (2022). https://doi.org/10.24018/ejeng.2022.7.3.2792
3. Liu, D., Xiao, J., Liu, J., Yuan, X., Zhang, S.: Dynamic energy trading and load scheduling algorithm for the end-user in smart grid. IEEE Access **8**, 189632–189645 (2020). https://doi.org/10.1109/ACCESS.2020.3031325
4. Paterakis, N.G., Catalao, J.P.S., Tascikaraoglu, A., Bakirtzis, A.G., Erdinc, O.: Demand response driven load pattern elasticity analysis for smart households. In: 2015 IEEE 5th International Conference on Power Engineering, Energy and Electrical Drives (POWERENG), Riga, Latvia, pp. 399–404. IEEE, May 2015. https://doi.org/10.1109/PowerEng.2015.7266350
5. Giordano, A., Mastroianni, C., Menniti, D., Pinnarelli, A., Scarcello, L., Sorrentino, N.: A two-stage approach for efficient power sharing within energy districts. IEEE Trans. Syst. Man Cybern. Syst. **51**(3), 1679–1689, March 2021. https://doi.org/10.1109/TSMC.2019.2902077
6. Li, H., Xiao, F., Yin, L., Wu, F.: Application of blockchain technology in energy trading: a review. Front. Energy Res. **9**, 671133 (2021). https://doi.org/10.3389/fenrg.2021.671133
7. Umar, A., Kumar, D., Ghose, T.: Peer-to-peer energy trading in a self-sustained microgrid system using blockchain technology. In: 2022 International Conference on IoT and Blockchain Technology (ICIBT), Ranchi, India, pp. 1–6. IEEE, May 2022. https://doi.org/10.1109/ICIBT52874.2022.9807741
8. Esmat, A., De Vos, M., Ghiassi-Farrokhfal, Y., Palensky, P., Epema, D.: A novel decentralized platform for peer-to-peer energy trading market with blockchain technology. Appl. Energy **282**, 116123 (2021). https://doi.org/10.1016/j.apenergy.2020.116123
9. Thukral, M.K.: Emergence of blockchain-technology application in peer-to-peer electrical-energy trading: a review. Clean Energy **5**(1), 104–123 (2021). https://doi.org/10.1093/ce/zkaa033
10. Rudd, S., Stapleton, L.: The transformation of peer-to-peer energy markets meta-analysis of state of the art and future trends. IFAC-PapersOnLine **55**(39), 1–8 (2022). https://doi.org/10.1016/j.ifacol.2022.12.001

11. AlSkaif, T., Crespo-Vazquez, J.L., Sekuloski, M., Van Leeuwen, G., Catalao, J.P.S.: Blockchain-based fully peer-to-peer energy trading strategies for residential energy systems. IEEE Trans. Ind. Inf. **18**(1), 231–241 (2022). https://doi.org/10.1109/TII.2021.3077008
12. Andoni, M., et al.: Blockchain technology in the energy sector: a systematic review of challenges and opportunities. Renew. Sustain. Energy Rev. **100**, 143–174 (2019). https://doi.org/10.1016/j.rser.2018.10.014
13. Bao, Z., Tang, C., Lin, F., Zheng, Z., Yu, X.: Rating-protocol optimization for blockchain-enabled hybrid energy trading in smart grids. Sci. China Inf. Sci. **66**(5), 159205 (2023). https://doi.org/10.1007/s11432-021-3390-7
14. Machacek, T., Biswal, M., Misra, S.: Proof of X: experimental insights on blockchain consensus algorithms in energy markets. In: 2021 IEEE Power & Energy Society Innovative Smart Grid Technologies Conference (ISGT), Washington, DC, USA, pp. 1–5. IEEE, February 2021. https://doi.org/10.1109/ISGT49243.2021.9372194
15. Abdella, J., Tari, Z., Anwar, A., Mahmood, A., Han, F.: An architecture and performance evaluation of blockchain-based peer-to-peer energy trading. IEEE Trans. Smart Grid **12**(4), 3364–3378 (2021). https://doi.org/10.1109/TSG.2021.3056147
16. Munoz, M.F., Zhang, K., Amara, F.: ZipZap: a blockchain solution for local energy trading. In: 2022 IEEE International Conference on Blockchain and Cryptocurrency (ICBC), Shanghai, China, pp. 1–5. IEEE, May 2022. https://doi.org/10.1109/ICBC54727.2022.9805486
17. Wang, N., Chau, S.C.-K.: Efficient off-chain micro-payment systems for blockchain-based P2P energy trading. In: Companion Proceedings of the 14th ACM International Conference on Future Energy Systems, Orlando, FL, USA. ACM, June 2023. https://doi.org/10.1145/3599733.3606299
18. Rousseau, D.M., Sitkin, S.B., Burt, R.S., Camerer, C.: Not so different after all: a cross-discipline view of trust. AMR **23**(3), 393–404 (1998). https://doi.org/10.5465/amr.1998.926617
19. Schilke, O., Reimann, M., Cook, K.S.: Trust in social relations. Annu. Rev. Sociol. **47**(1), 239–259 (2021). https://doi.org/10.1146/annurev-soc-082120-082850
20. Akerlof, G.A.: The market for "Lemons": quality uncertainty and the market mechanism. Q. J. Econ. **84**(3), 488 (1970). https://doi.org/10.2307/1879431
21. Morgan, R.M., Hunt, S.D.: The commitment-trust theory of relationship marketing. J. Mark. **58**(3), 20–38 (1994). https://doi.org/10.1177/002224299405800302
22. Pollitt, M.: The economics of trust, norms and networks. Bus. Ethics Eur. Rev. **11**(2), 119–128 (2002). https://doi.org/10.1111/1467-8608.00266
23. Dewar, K.: The value exchange: generating trust in the digital world. Bus. Inf. Rev. **34**(2), 96–100 (2017). https://doi.org/10.1177/0266382117711330
24. Barrane, F.Z., Ndubisi, N.O., Kamble, S., Karuranga, G.E., Poulin, D.: Building trust in multi-stakeholder collaborations for new product development in the digital transformation era. BIJ **28**(1), 205–228 (2021). https://doi.org/10.1108/BIJ-04-2020-0164
25. Baldwin, J.: In digital we trust: bitcoin discourse, digital currencies, and decentralized network fetishism. Palgrave Commun. **4**(1), 14 (2018). https://doi.org/10.1057/s41599-018-0065-0
26. Davidson, S., De Filippi, P., Potts, J.: Economics of blockchain. SSRN J. (2016). https://doi.org/10.2139/ssrn.2744751
27. Ølnes, S., Ubacht, J., Janssen, M.: Blockchain in government: benefits and implications of distributed ledger technology for information sharing. Gov. Inf. Q. **34**(3), 355–364 (2017). https://doi.org/10.1016/j.giq.2017.09.007
28. Werbach, K.: Trust, but verify: why the blockchain needs the law (2018). https://doi.org/10.15779/Z38H41JM9N
29. Nakamoto, S.: Bitcoin: a peer-to-peer electronic cash system. Cryptography Mailing list (2008). https://www.metzdowd.com/pipermail/cryptography/2008-October/014810.html. https://www.bitcoin.org/bitcoin.pdf

30. Finck, M.: Blockchains: regulating the unknown. Ger. Law J. **19**(4), 665–692 (2018). https://doi.org/10.1017/S2071832200022847

31. Hileman, G., Rauchs, M.: 2017 global blockchain benchmarking study. SSRN J. (2017). https://doi.org/10.2139/ssrn.3040224

32. Atzori, M.: Blockchain technology and decentralized governance: is the state still necessary? SSRN J. (2015). https://doi.org/10.2139/ssrn.2709713

33. Swan, M., de Filippi, P.: Toward a philosophy of blockchain: a symposium: introduction. Metaphilosophy **48**(5), 603–619 (2017). https://doi.org/10.1111/meta.12270

34. Christidis, K., Devetsikiotis, M.: Blockchains and smart contracts for the internet of things. IEEE Access **4**, 2292–2303 (2016). https://doi.org/10.1109/ACCESS.2016.2566339

35. Wright, A., De Filippi, P.: Decentralized blockchain technology and the rise of lex cryptographia. SSRN J. (2015). https://doi.org/10.2139/ssrn.2580664

36. Chowdhury, M.J.M., Colman, A., Kabir, M.A., Han, J., Sarda, P.: Blockchain versus database: a critical analysis. In: 2018 17th IEEE International Conference on Trust, Security and Privacy in Computing and Communications. In: 12th IEEE International Conference on Big Data Science and Engineering (TrustCom/BigDataSE), New York, NY, USA, pp. 1348–1353. IEEE, August 2018. https://doi.org/10.1109/TrustCom/BigDataSE.2018.00186

37. Sternberg, H.S., Hofmann, E., Roeck, D.: The struggle is real: insights from a supply chain blockchain case. J. Bus. Logist. **42**(1), 71–87 (2020). https://doi.org/10.1111/jbl.12240

38. Beck, R., Czepluch, J.S., Lollike, N., Malone, S.: Blockchain – the gateway to trust-free cryptographic transactions. In: Title of Host Publication Twenty-Fourth European Conference on Information Systems (ECIS), İstanbul, Turkey, pp. 1–14. Springer, Istanbul (2016). https://aisel.aisnet.org/ecis2016_rp/153/

39. Ishmaev, G.: Blockchain technology as an institution of property. Metaphilosophy **48**(5), 666–686 (2017). https://doi.org/10.1111/meta.12277

40. Glaser, F.: Pervasive decentralisation of digital infrastructures: a framework for blockchain enabled system and use case analysis. Presented at the Hawaii International Conference on System Sciences (2017). https://doi.org/10.24251/HICSS.2017.186

41. Hawlitschek, F., Notheisen, B., Teubner, T.: The limits of trust-free systems: a literature review on blockchain technology and trust in the sharing economy. Electron. Commer. Res. Appl. **29**, 50–63 (2018). https://doi.org/10.1016/j.elerap.2018.03.005

42. Hilal, A.A., Hilal, T.A., Hilal, H.A.: Investigating the failure of the blockchain technology and suggested recommendations. Procedia Comput. Sci. **224**, 450–455 (2023). https://doi.org/10.1016/j.procs.2023.09.063

43. Caldarelli, G., Rossignoli, C., Zardini, A.: Overcoming the blockchain oracle problem in the traceability of non-fungible products. Sustainability **12**(6), 2391 (2020). https://doi.org/10.3390/su12062391

44. Violino, S., et al.: A full technological traceability system for extra virgin olive oil. Foods **9**(5), 624 (2020). https://doi.org/10.3390/foods9050624

45. Longo, F., Nicoletti, L., Padovano, A., d'Atri, G., Forte, M.: Blockchain-enabled supply chain: an experimental study. Comput. Ind. Eng. **136**, 57–69 (2019). https://doi.org/10.1016/j.cie.2019.07.026

46. Zhang, A., Zhong, R.Y., Farooque, M., Kang, K., Venkatesh, V.G.: Blockchain-based life cycle assessment: an implementation framework and system architecture. Resour. Conserv. Recycl. **152**, 104512 (2020). https://doi.org/10.1016/j.resconrec.2019.104512

47. Wang, S., Li, D., Zhang, Y., Chen, J.: Smart contract-based product traceability system in the supply chain scenario. IEEE Access **7**, 115122–115133 (2019). https://doi.org/10.1109/ACCESS.2019.2935873

48. Westerkamp, M., Victor, F., Küpper, A.: Tracing manufacturing processes using blockchain-based token compositions. Digit. Commun. Netw. **6**(2), 167–176 (2020). https://doi.org/10.1016/j.dcan.2019.01.007

49. Dib, O., Brousmiche, K.-L., Durand, A., Thea, E., Hamida, E.B.: Consortium blockchains: overview, applications and challenges. Int. J. Adv. Telecommun. **11**(1–2) (2018). https://www.researchgate.net/publication/328887130_Consortium_Blockchains_O verview_Applications_and_Challenges

50. Viriyasitavat, W., Hoonsopon, D.: Blockchain characteristics and consensus in modern business processes. J. Ind. Inf. Integr. **13**, 32–39 (2019). https://doi.org/10.1016/j.jii.2018. 07.004

51. Attaran, M., Gunasekaran, A.: Blockchain-enabled technology: the emerging technology set to reshape and decentralise many industries. IJADS **12**(4), 424 (2019). https://doi.org/10. 1504/IJADS.2019.102642

52. Bodkhe, U., et al.: Blockchain for industry 4.0: a comprehensive review. IEEE Access **8**, 79764–79800 (2020). https://doi.org/10.1109/ACCESS.2020.2988579

53. Gobel, J., Krzesinski, A.E.: Increased block size and bitcoin blockchain dynamics. In: 2017 27th International Telecommunication Networks and Applications Conference (ITNAC), Melbourne, VIC, pp. 1–6. IEEE, November 2017. https://doi.org/10.1109/ATNAC.2017.821 5367

54. Al-Jaroodi, J., Mohamed, N.: Blockchain in industries: a survey. IEEE Access **7**, 36500–36515 (2019). https://doi.org/10.1109/ACCESS.2019.2903554

55. Casino, F., Kanakaris, V., Dasaklis, T.K., Moschuris, S., Rachaniotis, N.P.: Modeling food supply chain traceability based on blockchain technology. IFAC-PapersOnLine **52**(13), 2728–2733 (2019). https://doi.org/10.1016/j.ifacol.2019.11.620

56. The European Union Blockchain Observatory & Forum: Scalability, interoperability and sustainability of blockchains (2019). https://www.eublockchainforum.eu/sites/default/files/ reports/report_scalaibility_06_03_2019.pdf

57. Hepp, T., Sharinghousen, M., Ehret, P., Schoenhals, A., Gipp, B.: On-chain vs. off-chain storage for supply- and blockchain integration. Inf. Technol. **60**(5–6), 283–291 (2018). https:// doi.org/10.1515/itit-2018-0019

58. Del Monte, G., Pennino, D., Pizzonia, M.: Scaling blockchains without giving up decentralization and security: a solution to the blockchain scalability trilemma. In: Proceedings of the 3rd Workshop on Cryptocurrencies and Blockchains for Distributed Systems, London, United Kingdom, pp. 71–76. ACM, September 2020. https://doi.org/10.1145/3410699.3413800

59. Reno, S., Haque, M.: Solving blockchain trilemma using off-chain storage protocol. IET Inf. Secur. **17**(4), 681–702 (2023). https://doi.org/10.1049/ise2.12124

60. Xu, X., Weber, I., Staples, M.: Architecture for Blockchain Applications, 1st edn. Springer, Cham (2019). https://doi.org/10.1007/978-3-030-03035-3

61. Singhal, B., Dhameja, G., Panda, P.S.: Beginning Blockchain: a Beginner's Guide to Building Blockchain Solutions. Apress, New York (2018)

62. Zhang, X., et al.: Blockchain-based safety management system for the grain supply chain. IEEE Access **8**, 36398–36410 (2020). https://doi.org/10.1109/ACCESS.2020.2975415

63. Chi, L., Zhu, X.: Hashing techniques: a survey and taxonomy. ACM Comput. Surv. **50**(1), 1–36 (2018). https://doi.org/10.1145/3047307

64. Shahid, A., Almogren, A., Javaid, N., Al-Zahrani, F.A., Zuair, M., Alam, M.: Blockchain-based agri-food supply chain: a complete solution. IEEE Access **8**, 69230–69243 (2020). https://doi.org/10.1109/ACCESS.2020.2986257

65. Salah, K., Nizamuddin, N., Jayaraman, R., Omar, M.: Blockchain-based soybean traceability in agricultural supply chain. IEEE Access **7**, 73295–73305 (2019). https://doi.org/10.1109/ ACCESS.2019.2918000

66. Chowdhury, M.J.M., et al.: A comparative analysis of distributed ledger technology platforms. IEEE Access **7**, 167930–167943 (2019). https://doi.org/10.1109/ACCESS.2019.2953729

67. Rebello, G.A.F., Camilo, G.F., Guimarães, L.C.B., De Souza, L.A.C., Thomaz, G.A., Duarte, O.C.M.B.: A security and performance analysis of proof-based consensus protocols. Ann. Telecommun. **77**(7–8), 517–537 (2022). https://doi.org/10.1007/s12243-021-00896-2

68. Nair, P.R., Dorai, D.R.: Evaluation of performance and security of proof of work and proof of stake using blockchain. In: 2021 Third International Conference on Intelligent Communication Technologies and Virtual Mobile Networks (ICICV), Tirunelveli, India, pp. 279–283. IEEE, February 2021. https://doi.org/10.1109/ICICV50876.2021.9388487

69. Nicolas, H.: It will cost you nothing to "kill" a proof-of-stake crypto-currency. SSRN J. (2014). https://doi.org/10.2139/ssrn.2393940

70. Dinh, T.T.A., Wang, J., Chen, G., Liu, R., Ooi, B.C., Tan, K.-L.: BLOCKBENCH: a framework for analyzing private blockchains. In: Proceedings of the 2017 ACM International Conference on Management of Data, Chicago, Illinois, USA, pp. 1085–1100. ACM, May 2017. https://doi.org/10.1145/3035918.3064033

71. Ekparinya, P., Gramoli, V., Jourjon, G.: The attack of the clones against proof-of-authority (2019). https://doi.org/10.48550/ARXIV.1902.10244

72. Tan, E., Mahula, S., Crompvoets, J.: Blockchain governance in the public sector: a conceptual framework for public management. Gov. Inf. Q. **39**(1), 101625 (2022). https://doi.org/10.1016/j.giq.2021.101625

73. Helliar, C.V., Crawford, L., Rocca, L., Teodori, C., Veneziani, M.: Permissionless and permissioned blockchain diffusion. Int. J. Inf. Manage. **54**, 102136 (2020). https://doi.org/10.1016/j.ijinfomgt.2020.102136

74. Cui, P., Dixon, J., Guin, U., Dimase, D.: A blockchain-based framework for supply chain provenance. IEEE Access **7**, 157113–157125 (2019). https://doi.org/10.1109/ACCESS.2019.2949951

75. Mao, D., Wang, F., Hao, Z., Li, H.: Credit evaluation system based on blockchain for multiple stakeholders in the food supply chain. IJERPH **15**(8), 1627 (2018). https://doi.org/10.3390/ijerph15081627

76. Chan, K.Y., Abdullah, J., Shahid, A.: A framework for traceable and transparent supply chain management for agri-food sector in Malaysia using blockchain technology. IJACSA **10**(11) (2019). https://doi.org/10.14569/IJACSA.2019.0101120

77. Song, J.M., Sung, J., Park, T.: Applications of blockchain to improve supply chain traceability. Procedia Comput. Sci. **162**, 119–122 (2019). https://doi.org/10.1016/j.procs.2019.11.266

78. Behnke, K., Janssen, M.F.W.H.A.: Boundary conditions for traceability in food supply chains using blockchain technology. Int. J. Inf. Manage. **52**, 101969 (2020). https://doi.org/10.1016/j.ijinfomgt.2019.05.025

79. Mirabelli, G., Solina, V.: Blockchain and agricultural supply chains traceability: research trends and future challenges. Procedia Manuf. **42**, 414–421 (2020). https://doi.org/10.1016/j.promfg.2020.02.054

80. Sund, T., Lööf, C., Nadjm-Tehrani, S., Asplund, M.: Blockchain-based event processing in supply chains—a case study at IKEA. Rob. Comput.-Integr. Manuf. **65**, 101971 (2020). https://doi.org/10.1016/j.rcim.2020.101971

81. Sidorov, M., Ong, M.T., Sridharan, R.V., Nakamura, J., Ohmura, R., Khor, J.H.: Ultra-lightweight mutual authentication RFID protocol for blockchain enabled supply chains. IEEE Access **7**, 7273–7285 (2019). https://doi.org/10.1109/ACCESS.2018.2890389

82. Saberi, S., Kouhizadeh, M., Sarkis, J., Shen, L.: Blockchain technology and its relationships to sustainable supply chain management. Int. J. Prod. Res. **57**(7), 2117–2135 (2019). https://doi.org/10.1080/00207543.2018.1533261

83. Gervais, A., Karame, G., Capkun, S., Capkun, V.: Is bitcoin a decentralized currency? Cryptology ePrint Archive, vol. 2013, no. 829 (2013). https://eprint.iacr.org/2013/829

Inspecting Bridges and Critical Infrastructure: An AI and Blockchain Approach

Adriano Mancini(✉) and Alessandro Galdelli

VRAI Lab - Università Politecnica delle Marche, Ancona, Italy
a.mancini@staff.univpm.it
https://www.vrailab.it

Abstract. In recent years, the safety and integrity of bridges and critical infrastructure have become a paramount concern for governments and societies worldwide. Traditional inspection methods are often time-consuming, prone to human error, and can be economically taxing. The advent of advanced technologies such as Artificial Intelligence (AI) and blockchain offers a transformative approach to inspecting and maintaining these structures. In this extended abstract we discuss the perspective and opportunities presented by integrating AI and blockchain in the inspection of bridges and critical infrastructure, emphasizing the enhancement of data integrity and the potential for these technologies to revolutionize the field.

Keywords: Infrastructure monitoring · Artificial Intelligence · Blockchain Technologies · Dependable Computing

1 Introduction

AI, particularly in the form of machine learning and computer vision, presents unprecedented opportunities for the inspection of bridges and critical infrastructure. Autonomous robots (also drones) equipped with cameras and AI-based analysis software can conduct visual inspections, reaching areas that are challenging and hazardous for human inspectors [5]. AI algorithms can analyze images and videos to detect cracks [1,3], corrosion [4], and other structural anomalies [10] with a level of precision and speed unattainable by human inspectors reducing the risk of human error. The capability to deploy autonomous robots opens new scenarios in this context. Robots can work in critical environments reducing the exposition to risks for human workers. A critical point in this scenario is the ability of robots to recover from faults ensuring the safety of all (workers, end-users, infrastructures). Several aspects should be considered in this case and the analysis of risks is a fundamental step that must be considered.

The use of robots could be cost effective and AI-driven robotic inspections can be conducted more frequently and at a fraction of the cost of traditional methods.

B. Sangchoolie et al. (Eds.): EDCC 2024 Workshops, CCIS 2078, pp. 123–126, 2024.
https://doi.org/10.1007/978-3-031-56776-6_12

The capability to acquire large amount of data (e.g. images, acceleration time-series) sets a new requirement for the data processing. Human operators can not analyze image by image so AI algorithms should support the decisions of experts providing warning where potential issues are detected. In Fig. 1 it is possible to see an examples of defect related to bridge inspection together with two junctions of panels.

Fig. 1. An example of image with two objects of interest. The junction of two panels by a soldering (not a issue) and a spot in the bottom-right corner (potential issue).

At this stage two main questions arises. The first question is related to the performance of machine learning models to detect defects in precise and accurate way. The second aspect is related to the decision of expert according to defects detected by AI algorithms.

Regarding the first point the capability to detect known and unknown defects is still an open research challenge even if interesting anomaly detection approaches have been recently proposed [9]. One of the main problem is the lack of dataset with different defects over different environmental conditions. Generative Adversarial Networks (GANs) can be considered as a valid and modern approach to generate high-quality images with defect for engineering purposes [6].

Regarding the second aspect it is necessary to ensure that the decisions of experts are tracked and certified for future audits. It is important at this stage to ensure that a proper package of data is created when a problem/issue is confirmed by experts or on the opposite side discarded due to a false positive detection.

2   The Potential Role of Blockchain: Centralized and Decentralized AI

While AI can significantly enhance the inspection process, ensuring the integrity, security, and transparency of the collected data is crucial. This is where blockchain technology comes into play. A blockchain is a decentralized, distributed ledger that records transactions in a secure, tamper-evident manner. Integrating blockchain technology with AI-driven inspection systems can offer several benefits:

- **Immutable Records**: once data (e.g., inspection reports, maintenance records) is recorded on a blockchain, it cannot be altered or deleted. This ensures the integrity of the data and builds trust among stakeholders.
- **Transparency and Traceability**: blockchain's transparent nature allows all stakeholders, including government bodies, construction companies, and the public, to trace the history of inspections and maintenance actions.
- **Security**: blockchain's decentralized nature makes it less vulnerable to hacks and unauthorized alterations, protecting sensitive infrastructure data from cyber threats.

In [8] authors discuss about the centralized and decentralized AI. A significant concern with centralized AI systems is the risk of data compromise, given that the data is consolidated and stored centrally, rendering it prone to hacking and tampering. Additionally, the verification of data origins and authenticity is not inherently assured in such setups. This vulnerability can result in AI decisions that are not only inaccurate but also potentially perilous and hazardous.

Decentralized AI operates by distributing processing, analysis, and decision-making across a network, leveraging trusted, digitally authenticated, and securely shared data transacted and preserved on the blockchain. This method functions in a dispersed and decentralized fashion, negating the necessity for trusted intermediaries or third-party facilitators.

2.1   Integrating AI and Blockchain: A Synergistic Approach

The integration of AI and blockchain in the inspection of bridges and critical infrastructure represents a synergistic approach that leverages the strengths of both technologies. AI enhances the efficiency and accuracy of inspections, while blockchain ensures the integrity and transparency of the inspection data. This integration can lead to a more proactive and data-driven approach to infrastructure maintenance, ultimately enhancing public safety and trust. Several approaches have been evaluated and tested in Industry4.0 scenarios as reported in [7].

Of course AI-Powered blockchain is another focus point that must be considered to implement in the future efficient decentralized architectures [11] considering also federated learning [2].

3   The Potential Role of Dependable Computing

Incorporating dependable computing into the AI and blockchain-driven inspection of bridges and critical infrastructure is crucial. It ensures not only the integrity and transparency of data but also the reliability, availability, and security of the inspection systems. As we move towards more technologically advanced methods of infrastructure inspection, the principles of dependable computing will play a pivotal role in shaping resilient, trustworthy systems that stakeholders can rely on for the safety and maintenance of critical structures.

Acknowledgements. This work has been developed in the context of TRUST-RISE project that received funding from the European Union's Horizon 2020 research and innovation program under the Marie Skłodowska-Curie grant agreement No. 101007820. This publication reflects only the author's view, and the REA is not responsible for any use that may be made of the information it contains. The authors want to thank Eng. Ferdinando Cannella, Head of Industrial Robotic Unit at Italian Institute of Technology for his support on smart inspection of bridges using AI and mobile robotics.

Disclosure of Interests. The authors have no competing interests to declare that are relevant to the content of this article.

References

1. Arafin, P., Billah, A.M., Issa, A.: Deep learning-based concrete defects classification and detection using semantic segmentation. Struct. Health Monit. **23**(1), 383–409 (2024). https://doi.org/10.1177/14759217231168212
2. Chhetri, B., Gopali, S., Olapojoye, R., Dehbash, S., Namin, A.S.: A survey on blockchain-based federated learning and data privacy (2023)
3. Sales da Cunha, B., das Chagas Moura, M., Souto Maior, C., Cláudia Negreiros, A., Didier Lins, I.: A comparison between computer vision- and deep learning-based models for automated concrete crack detection. Proc. Inst. Mech. Eng. Part O: J. Risk and Reliabil. **237**(5), 994–1010 (2023). https://doi.org/10.1177/1748006X221140966
4. Das, A., Ichi, E., Dorafshan, S.: Image-based corrosion detection in ancillary structures. Infrastructures **8**(4) (2023). https://doi.org/10.3390/infrastructures8040066
5. Galdelli, A., et al.: A novel remote visual inspection system for bridge predictive maintenance. Remote Sens. **14**(9) (2022). https://doi.org/10.3390/rs14092248
6. Han, C., Ma, T., Huyan, J., Tong, Z., Yang, H., Yang, Y.: Multi-stage generative adversarial networks for generating pavement crack images. Eng. Appl. Artif. Intell. **131**, 107767 (2024). https://doi.org/10.1016/j.engappai.2023.107767
7. Javaid, M., Haleem, A., Pratap Singh, R., Khan, S., Suman, R.: Blockchain technology applications for industry 4.0: a literature-based review. blockchain. Res. Appl. **2**(4), 100027 (2021). https://doi.org/10.1016/j.bcra.2021.100027
8. Kuznetsov, O., Sernani, P., Romeo, L., Frontoni, E., Mancini, A.: On the integration of artificial intelligence and blockchain technology: a perspective about security. IEEE Access **12**, 3881–3897 (2024). https://doi.org/10.1109/ACCESS.2023.3349019
9. Liu, J., et al.: Deep industrial image anomaly detection: a survey. Mach. Intell. Res. **21**(1), 104–135 (2024). https://doi.org/10.1007/s11633-023-1459-z
10. Qu, C., Zhang, H., Zhang, R., Zou, S., Huang, L., Li, H.: Multiclass anomaly detection of bridge monitoring data with data migration between different bridges for balancing data. Appl. Sci. **13**(13) (2023). https://doi.org/10.3390/app13137635
11. Soori, M., Dastres, R., Arezoo, B.: Ai-powered blockchain technology in industry 4.0, a review. J. Econ. Technol. (2024). https://doi.org/10.1016/j.ject.2024.01.001

TRUST IN BLOCKCHAIN Short Paper

On the Use of Decentralized Ledger Technologies for Dynamic Radio Management of NB-IoT 5G

Jose Rubio-Hernan[1](✉) ⓘ, Juan J. Alcaraz[2] ⓘ, and Joaquin Garcia-Alfaro[1] ⓘ

[1] SAMOVAR, Télécom SudParis, Institut Polytechnique de Paris, Palaiseau, France
{rubio_he,garcia_a}@telecom-sudparis.eu
[2] Department of Information and Communication Technologies, Universidad Politécnica de Cartagena, Murcia, Spain
juan.alcaraz@upct.es

Keywords: Dynamic Spectrum Sharing (DSS) · Cooperative Spectrum Sharing (CSS) · Narrowband IoT (NB-IoT) · 5G Networks · Low Power Wide Area Network (LPWAN) · Token Management · Decentralization · Decentralized Ledger Technologies (DLT) · Blockchain Technology (BCT)

NB-IoT 5G (Narrowband Internet of Things for 5G) networks is an LPWAN (Low Power Wide Area Network) communication standard created for the management of IoT systems with low power consumption, i.e., systems with extremely high latency, in the order of seconds, and very limited data rates [1]. One of the important problems in these networks is the management of the spectrum in an optimized and dynamic manner [2, 4, 5].

We aim at exploring how to handle the problem of spectrum management on NB-IoT 5G network, when several operators coexist in the same geographic area. For instance, when one operator has the primary license to use the spectrum and the others make controlled use of some carriers shared by the primary operator.

Current literature shows solutions handling the aforementioned problem by using of Decentralized Ledger Technologies (DLT) [3]. One of the advantages of the DLT approach is the enforcement of integrity of radio spectrum management on NB-IoT 5G network in case of dynamic changes in operators' needs. For instance, the primary operator could reduce the maximum tolerated power level or even temporarily disable access to its spectrum in high-traffic situations. The idea is to use a system of layers of verification of such integrity, starting from the lowest layer in ms (ensuring fast and secure communication). This would be included in the decentralized part of this communication model between NB-IoT 5G operators'. It is worth noting that the aforementioned idea combined with Cooperative Spectrum Sharing (CSS) [6] allows us to orchestrate the interoperability between several operators in specific geographic areas.

To carry out the above proposition, we need to configure transmission control protocols to operate in a CSS scenario: 1) Access protocols; 2) Interval transmission protocols; 3) Transmission protocols under controlled interference conditions; or even 4) exploiting features already present in NB-IoT such as

B. Sangchoolie et al. (Eds.): EDCC 2024 Workshops, CCIS 2078, pp. 129–130, 2024.
https://doi.org/10.1007/978-3-031-56776-6

transmitting with low power but many consecutive repetitions, both downlink and uplink. Likewise, we need to create one or several tokens to handle, using DLT, the spectrum management into an NB-IoT 5G network between the different operators. Cooperative spectrum sharing tokens, based on smart contracts, must allow revocation, expiration, and sharing periods, among other functionalities. The goal is to allow optimal and agreed management between the operators. As well as, a transmission control protocol that allows the optimization of the spectrum without affecting the quality of the service.

Discussion on open challenges and future directions for research will cover, as well, existing advantages and limitations on the use of decentralization technologies on NB-IoT 5G, such as incentive mechanisms for the automation of spectrum frequency auctions [7].

Acknowledgments. We acknowledge support from the European Union's Horizon 2020 research and innovation programme under the Marie Skłodowska-Curie grant agreement No. 101007820. Authors acknowledge as well Grant PID2020-116329GB-C22 funded by MCIN/AEI/10.13039/501100011033.

Disclaimer. This article reflects only the authors' view and the REA (Research Executive Agency) is not responsible for any use that may be made of the information it contains.

References

1. 3GPP. Release 17 of 3GPP (2022). www.3gpp.org/specifications-technologies/releases/release-17
2. Hassan, M.B., et al.: An enhanced cooperative communication scheme for physical uplink shared channel in NB-IoT. Wireless Pers. Commun. 1–20 (2021)
3. Liang, Y.-C.: Dynamic Spectrum Management. SCT, Springer, Singapore (2020). https://doi.org/10.1007/978-981-15-0776-2
4. Muteba, F., Djouani, K., Olwal, T.O.: Challenges and Solutions of Spectrum Allocation in NB-IoT Technology. Tshwane University of Technology, Pretoria (2020)
5. Muteba, K., Djouani, K., Olwal, T.: 5G NB-IoT: design, considerations, solutions and challenges. Procedia Comput. Sci. **198**, 86–93 (2022)
6. Qian, B., et al.: Multi-operator spectrum sharing for massive IoT coexisting in 5G/B5G wireless networks. IEEE J. Sel. Areas Commun. **39**(3), 881–895 (2021). https://doi.org/10.1109/JSAC.2020.3018803
7. Zhang, Y., Lee, C., Niyato, D., Wang, P.: Auction approaches for resource allocation in wireless systems: a survey. IEEE Commun. Surv. Tutor. **15**(3), 1020–1041 (2012)

Author Index

B. Sangchoolie et al. (Eds.): EDCC 2024 Workshops, CCIS 2078, p. 131, 2024.
https://doi.org/10.1007/978-3-031-56776-6

Printed in the United States
by Baker & Taylor Publisher Services